GENESIS
OF ORIGINAL
INTENT

ENDORSEMENTS

"This book is filled with Scripture, which, put together, reveals God's intent for the world He created and the people He placed in it to carry out His purposes. What were these purposes? Why are we here? How do we fit into God's original design? Was all lost in the Garden when men sinned and broke fellowship with God and brought disobedience and darkness into the perfect creation? Is it important to know God's original design, since all appeared to be lost? How does God see us now? Who does He say we are, and what does He want us to do? What is the role of the Church today? The coming of a Savior was the answer to man's sin and 'paradise lost.' Read on to see how God's original intent for creation and for us as His people is key to understanding His purposes for us in these end times."

ANN ANDERSON
Prophetic Intercessor and Friend

"Leah Dent has written an anointed treatise on how she learned, and how you can learn, to hear God's voice and discover His original design and purpose for man. She shows by personal experience how to apply what you've learned to your life, your culture, and the world around you. Leah shares many interesting biblical truths, like what makes up the soul, in an easy-to-grasp way. She explains and exhorts believers to move in the gifts of the Spirit and make disciples. This book contains much value for those who seek a deeper walk with God and His guidance. She encourages believers to listen for His voice, follow His directions, and become His holy temple on earth."

ELVA MARTIN
Author, Retired Minister

"In Acts 16:6-10, Paul and Silas and Timothy are on their missionary journeys, and the Holy Spirit forbids them to go to two different places and then gives Paul a vision to go to Macedonia. I have known Leah for many years and have watched her live the same way. She goes where the Spirit tells her to go and does what the Spirit tells her to do prophetically. I say this to say that what she has to teach has considerable experience behind it and is not just an intellectual exercise. I am quick to add, however, that she is careful to back up everything that she says with the Word, which she considers the plumb line to every Christian's life. I highly recommend her book as a valuable addition to anyone's library to encourage them to follow God's original intent for their lives. I, myself, was both convicted and encouraged."

DAVID A. MCCANN MDIV., MD

GENESIS
OF ORIGINAL
INTENT

Leah Augustine Dent

An in-depth look at what Scripture says about God's original intent for mankind in relationship to Himself.

AMBASSADOR INTERNATIONAL
GREENVILLE, SOUTH CAROLINA & BELFAST, NORTHERN IRELAND

www.ambassador-international.com

Genesis of Original Intent
An In-Depth Look at What Scripture Says About God's Original Intent for Mankind in Relationship to Himself
©2022 by Leah Augustine Dent
All rights reserved

ISBN: 978-1-64960-042-4
eISBN: 978-1-64960-043-1

Cover Design by Hannah Linder Designs
Interior Typesetting by Dentelle Design

Unless otherwise marked, Scripture taken from the New American Standard Bible 1995® (NASB1995), Copyright © 1960, 1971, 1977, 1995 by The Lockman Foundation. All rights reserved.

Scripture from the King James Version taken from the Public Domain.

Scripture marked TPT taken from The Passion Translation®. Copyright © 2017, 2018, 2020 by Passion & Fire Ministries, Inc. Used by permission. All rights reserved.

No part of this publication may be reproduced, distributed, or transmitted in any form or by any means, including photocopying, recording, or other electronic or mechanical methods, without the prior written permission of the publisher, except in the case of brief quotations embodied in critical reviews and certain other non-commercial uses permitted by copyright law. For permission requests, contact the publisher using the information below.

AMBASSADOR INTERNATIONAL
Emerald House
411 University Ridge, Suite B14
Greenville, SC 29601
United States
www.ambassador-international.com

AMBASSADOR BOOKS
The Mount
2 Woodstock Link
Belfast, BT6 8DD
Northern Ireland, United Kingdom
www.ambassadormedia.co.uk

The colophon is a trademark of Ambassador, a Christian publishing company.

This book is dedicated to all the godly pastors who have played a part in teaching me and giving me a love for the Word of God. I have been so blessed to be taught by you from the time I was able to sit in a pew. It is also dedicated to many spiritual leaders in the body of Christ who helped me grow into coupling the Word of God with the things of the Holy Spirit. I have benefited from your many teachings and your encouragement to go deeper into the things of the Lord and into my prophetic gifting. Thank you all.

TABLE OF CONTENTS

INTRODUCTION   11

CHAPTER 1
IN THE BEGINNING   13

CHAPTER 2
NAKED AND NOT ASHAMED   17

CHAPTER 3
IS MY WORD   29

CHAPTER 4
ALL ROADS LEAD TO ROME   33

CHAPTER 5
SPIRIT, SOUL, AND BODY   41

CHAPTER 6
IN OUR IMAGE   49

CHAPTER 7
A SUITABLE HELPER   55

CHAPTER 8
FEARFULLY AND WONDERFULLY MADE   63

CHAPTER 9
ANOTHER BEGINNING   69

CHAPTER 10
GOD'S INTENT FOR INDIVIDUALS 77

CHAPTER 11
TEMPLES OF THE LIVING GOD 87

CHAPTER 12
THE BIBLE: OUR PLUMB LINE 97

CHAPTER 13
EQUIPPING CENTERS 107

CHAPTER 14
RESTORING AMERICA TO HER ORIGINAL ROOTS 111

EPILOGUE 121

BIBLIOGRAPHY 123

DISCOGRAPHY 127

INTRODUCTION

"Genesis of original intent" is quite a phrase. What exactly does it mean? Good question—one I asked myself for several months after that phrase was spoken over my life by a conference speaker. I pondered this and prayed about it but came up with nothing. How did God want to apply this phrase to my life? What did this phrase mean to me, since it had been spoken as a word of knowledge to me through this conference speaker? I take these words seriously and didn't want to miss what God was saying to me. To be honest with you, I am still pondering the totality of this phrase.

The notes in my Hebrew-Greek Key Study Bible for Genesis state, "More than half of human history is covered in its scant fifty chapters. Genesis answers our gnawing questions about the origins of the universe, of ourselves, of all life forms, of sin and evils in the world."

To help me—and you—understand what the Lord is saying in this phrase, let's look at each word individually. According to the introduction of Genesis in the Zondervan New American Study Bible, "The English title Genesis, is Greek in origin and comes from the word *geneseos*. which appears in the Greek translation (Septuagint) of 2:4; 5:1. Depending on its context, the word can mean 'birth,' 'genealogy,' or 'history of origin.'" In the Hebrew text, the phrase "In the beginning" is *re'shiyth*, which is the first phrase of the book of Genesis.[1] Both words imply the beginning of something.

---

1 *Blue Letter Bible*, s.v., "re'shiyth," www.blueletterbible.org/lang/Lexicon/Lexicon.cfm?strongs=H7225&t=KJV (accessed July 1, 2019).

The word *original* as an adjective means "present or existing from the beginning; first or earliest; created directly and personally by an artist; not a copy or imitation; not dependent on other people's ideas; inventive and unusual."[2]

The word *intent* as a noun means "intention or purpose."[3]

Before anything else existed, God did. He was present from the very beginning of time. There is no marker for when He became; He just was. God's intention from the beginning was . . . what? Let's put this all together and see what we come up with. It is like adding in ingredient after ingredient to a recipe and seeing how it all comes out in the end. As we add the meaning of these words together one by one, what do they say based on their meaning? The "genesis of original intent" could read, "The origin or beginning for a purpose created directly, personally, and originally by God."

When something is created, it is usually created for a single purpose; later, it may evolve and become usable in another way. Take a toothbrush, for example. Its original intent is to brush teeth. However, I have been known to save old ones to use to scrub in tight places, but that is not why it was created. Recently, I found myself taking my trusty, old toothbrush and using it to get lint out of my dryer in a difficult-to-reach place. Same concept with a cup—it is created for people to drink from, but again, I have been known to use it to bale water out of somewhere I didn't want it to be. Often, I use a cup to water my potted plants. Even though things evolve to be used in other ways, the designer of them created them to be used in a certain way.

In the chapters of this book, I will start to unfold what I believe the Lord showed me this phrase means as it unfolds first to me and then, hopefully, to you.

---

2   Bing.com, *s.v.*, "original," www.bing.com/search?q=original+meaning&form (accessed July 1, 2019).
3   Bing.com, *s.v.*, "intent," www.bing.com/search?q=intent+meaning&form (accessed July 1, 2019).

CHAPTER 1

IN THE BEGINNING

Most people—and I would hope all Christians—are familiar with the phrase, "In the beginning." It is the opening words of the Holy Bible. The full sentence reads, "In the beginning God created the heavens and the earth." Hebrews 1:10 says almost the same thing: "And, 'YOU, LORD, IN THE BEGINNING LAID THE FOUNDATION OF THE EARTH, AND THE HEAVENS ARE THE WORK OF YOUR HAND.'"

At the very onset of time, before mankind existed, God created the heavens and the earth. When God created the heavens and the earth, they were in perfect alignment with each other. The Earth, the sun, and the moon were all in the proper positions that the Creator of the universe put them in. No big bang could have lined all of these things up the way they are without the Earth either burning up by being a couple of degrees closer to the sun or freezing over by being a couple of degrees farther way from the sun. All of creation was originally in alignment with God's genesis of original intent and the purpose for which He created it.

Psalm 104 is full of how God established the heavens and earth. Psalm 104:5 says, "He established the earth upon its foundations, so that it will not totter forever and ever." This verse shows clearly how the God of the universe has aligned the cosmos in perfection. It should not—it cannot—move one degree from where He placed it without His permission. Verses six through nine speak of the boundaries of the sea and how the mountains and the valleys are established:

> You covered it with the deep as with a garment;
> The waters were standing above the mountains.
> At Your rebuke they fled,
> At the sound of Your thunder they hurried away.
> The mountains rose; the valleys sank down
> To the place which You established for them.
> You set a boundary that they may not pass over,
> So that they will not return to cover the earth.

Verse nineteen tells of how the moon and sun know their places: "He made the moon for the seasons; the sun knows the place of its setting."

Psalm 33:6-9 further establishes God's providence and perfect alignment in creation:

> By the word of the LORD the heavens were made,
> And by the breath of His mouth all their host.
> He gathers the waters of the sea together as a heap;
> He lays up the deeps in storehouses.
> Let all the earth fear the LORD;
> Let all the inhabitants of the world stand in awe of Him
> For He spoke, and it was done;
> He commanded, and it stood fast.

When a builder builds a new structure, it must be "plumb." A plumb line is defined as "a weight on the end of a line, used especially by masons and carpenters to establish a true vertical."[4] If a building is not built in a "plumb" fashion, it will not be safe and may not stand the test of time. No builder with any integrity would build a building that was not in perfect "plumb." When God created the heavens and the earth, He made everything to be in perfect alignment according to His purposes and plans before the foundation of the world was laid.

As I looked intently at Genesis 1, I could picture God standing back like an artist looking at a canvas that he had just painted to see whether he approved

---

4   *The Free Dictionary*, s.v. "plomb," www.thefreedictionary.com/plomb (accessed July 1, 2019).

of it or not. I get this picture when I read where the Scripture says He looked at what He had created, and it was good. The heavens and the earth—and all that they contain—are the largest, greatest canvases ever created. They are masterpieces beyond any masterpiece painted or sculpted by some of the greatest artists who have ever lived. Da Vinci's *Mona Lisa* or his *Last Supper* or Michelangelo's Sistine Chapel or statue of *David*, as magnificent as they are, cannot begin to compare to a raging sea, or the Alps, or a glorious sunset over the ocean. Heaven and earth, animals, foliage of all kinds, plant life, human beings, and on and on are all part of God's masterful creation. Everything God ever designed and spoke into being is the best of the best—the "Top Gun," so to speak—not just in beauty but in how it all functions in complete harmony. Our world was, at one time, ecologically in complete balance. Our bodies, such intricate machines, functioned in absolute perfection before Adam and Eve ate the forbidden fruit. All of creation, each and every piece of it, was in alignment with God's genesis of original intent. Until . . .

HISTORY CHANGED IN THE GARDEN

God's perfect world changed in one moment of time, by one single act of rebellion. Eve took the fruit, ate it, and gave it to Adam to eat. When they ate it, their eyes were opened to good and evil. Prior to this, they had no frame of reference for anything evil. They had only known the goodness of God. They now understood what it meant to be naked. Shame became a part of their souls. God judged what they did, and life as we know it today became a reality in one short moment in time. Religion could now replace relationship because man was now free to choose worshiping idols and empty traditions of men, instead of having a "walk in the garden" relationship with the Father.

Things only were thrown out of balance through man's sin. In her book *Christianity is Jewish*, Edith Schaeffer stated that after the fall of mankind "the universe became abnormal."[5] She is exactly right in that statement; what

---

5   Edith Schaeffer, *Christianity is Jewish* (Wheaton: Tyndale House Publishers, Inc, 1975), 33.

was originally meant to be was no longer going to be as God intended it to be. Death had entered the universe that had so beautifully and intricately been created by the most brilliant Creator ever; and with it came disorder, disharmony, sin, sickness, hate, greed, and all manner of evil ultimately leading to death.

Our world is no longer ecologically in balance because of what mankind has done to it. What God created in perfection is now a muddled mess because of man's original sin. Mankind took a brush full of black paint and, thinking he was perfecting the original painting, wielded it to God's perfect canvas and marred it for all time. He took a mallet to the greatest sculptures ever created—man and woman—and desecrated them with sin. Even the fittest and healthiest human being is still in a state of perpetual dying because of the one willful act of the first two people God created, Adam and Eve. What was His original intent for these two and everyone to come after them? Let's look at Scripture and see.

CHAPTER 2

NAKED AND NOT ASHAMED

Before the fall of mankind, Adam and Eve shared an unparalleled relationship with their Creator. Did you know that God loved to garden? Look at Genesis 2:8: "The LORD God planted a garden toward the east, in Eden . . ." He planted the garden. I'm sure it was not like we plant gardens, but nonetheless, it says He planted it. He didn't order anyone else to do it; He did it Himself. I wish I could see what that original garden looked like. I am sure the beauty of it was breathtaking. I have been to many beautiful botanical gardens over the years and have the pictures to prove it; but as beautiful as they are, it would be like comparing a toad to a prince in light of the beauty of Eden to other gardens.

In the middle of this garden, God placed Adam, as the rest of Genesis 2:8 states: "And there He placed the man whom He had formed." He could have put him in a desert or on a tropical island, a mountain top or a valley, but He didn't. He put him in a garden. The very one He planted Himself. Now if you are going to plant a garden, what do you put in it? Personally, I would plant the things I love the most. I am not going to choose plants I don't care for; I am going to choose those that I find the prettiest or most interesting. God had a big advantage over my garden options. He had perfect soil to plant in, perfect weather to plant by, and access to the most stunning plants ever. And if He hadn't already created them, all He had to do was speak, and they would exist. It says of the trees that they were pleasing to the sight and good for food, and a river flowed through the Garden. This was a garden extraordinaire! Can you imagine waking up to that day after day? In real estate, location is everything. This was the ultimate location to live in. The views would have been breathtaking. This was prime real estate.

I can't be sure, but by the sound of the text, the Garden was also home to many of the animals. It says that God formed the animals and brought them to the man (Adam) to name. I can't imagine them then being sent out of the Garden to live after Adam named them, tended them, and had complete dominion over them. I am an animal lover, so to not only have beautiful trees and plants with luscious fruit on them surrounding me with a river running through it all but to also have this magical place teeming with animals would have truly been heaven here on earth. That would have been my forever happy place. But it gets better!

We have no idea how long Adam and Eve lived this idyllic life in the Garden together, sharing it with their Creator. The Scripture doesn't tell us. It could have been one year or one hundred years—or just one day. Probably a shorter time period because Eve had not born any children yet. After they sinned, Adam and Eve heard God walking in the Garden in the cool of the day, so it is plausible, even likely, that they enjoyed this kind of intimate fellowship with their Creator quite often, possibly daily. I can only imagine how wonderful that would have been.

The Garden must have been quite huge; after all, a river ran through it. Not just an ordinary backyard, garden variety kind of garden (no pun intended). There were probably so many elements of this garden to be discovered by Adam and Eve on their walks with the Lord. Remember, they were new creations—as was everything that had just been created—so, it all was waiting for their discovery of it. I could just picture the Lord pulling back a leaf on a plant and exposing to them something else remarkable below the leaf. There were all manner of plant life to discover, as well as species of bugs and animals. It is really unimaginable what it must have been like.

As a child, I loved to go mushroom hunting with my father in the spring when the morel mushrooms would pop their wrinkled heads above the surface of the ground. You had to have a keen eye to find them as they blended in with the ground and often hid underneath the fallen leaves from the year before. The growing season for them was short, and the conditions for them to appear had to be just right. This would have been the type of experience Adam and Eve had with the Lord as He peeled back things on the surface to show them things hidden underneath.

One year, I took biology in summer school, and we were taken to a local lake to discover the little creatures that inhabited the area around the lake. One tiny, little, fishlike thing we discovered could have its head cut in two, and it would then grow two heads. They could have had a lifetime of learning and discovering these kind of garden secrets if they hadn't been banished from the Garden. As beautiful as the Garden was, and as perfect as the weather must have been, the most blessed thing of all would have been to experience that kind of unhindered relationship with the one and only Creator of heaven and earth.

After eating the forbidden fruit, they realized they were naked. They had no concept of being naked prior to this. Have you ever had a naked dream? I have; it makes me shudder to think about. I hate those dreams where I am out in public and completely naked. They make me feel dirty or vulnerable, at the very least. In these dreams, at times, I am trying to hide my nakedness from the other people in the dream. That is what Adam and Eve were doing, trying to hide their nakedness from the only other Person in the Garden—God.

On some of my mission trips to one particular South American country, women were under a spirit of shame. Many of them were sexually abused as children, and they walked around with the shame of it almost visible on them. When they would come to me for prayer, they would not look me in the eyes, but their heads were always bowed down—not out of respect but out of shame. My first prayer for these women was to break off shame. While they carried shame around their necks like an albatross, they were not free to receive ministry in any other form. Over and over, I put my hand under their chins and lifted their heads to look at me. I spoke to the shame to leave them and affirmed to them that they were loved by the Lord and that none of this was His will. Shame had to be dealt with first before I could minister to them in other ways. This was the underlying cause of most of their problems for which they wanted prayer. It was such a joy to see the difference in these women once the darkness of shame had been removed from them. Their whole countenance would change, and they would no longer hang their heads but instead walked with their heads held high and a smile on their faces.

Adam and Eve were naked in the Garden. They had no clothes on to cover them or to bind them. We all know, at times, how binding and uncomfortable clothing can be. Their being naked was depicted in the physical sense, but metaphorically speaking, there was nothing between them and their God—nothing was hidden behind a layer of cloth, literally or metaphorically. It was all out there for God to see. It was after God created Adam and Eve that He said His creation was very good. He liked what He saw. The man and woman He fashioned from the dust were very good, even naked. As far as God was concerned, Adam and Eve were perfect. They were His "very good" creation, and they were probably the most handsome couple ever when they were first created, as no sin had yet entered the world.

The King James Version of the Bible tells us in Revelation 4:11, "Thou art worthy, O Lord, to receive glory and honour and power: for thou hast created all things, and for thy pleasure they are and were created." God wanted us for Himself. He made us to have unfettered fellowship with Him, with nothing standing in between Him and us, not even clothing. God, Who could have anything He wanted just by speaking it into existence, wanted you and me for

His pleasure. His original intent for mankind was to fellowship unhindered whenever He wanted to. God wanted us to enjoy fellowship with Him as well. It wasn't to be just one-sided. It was always about intimacy with Him and never about religion. He created us to have a regular intimate relationship with Him with nothing in between Him and us. That was the genesis of His original intent for mankind!

It was always about relationship; it was never about religious icons or empty rituals, or even about belonging to a religious organization. It is not about lighting candles or wearing crosses as jewelry. It is about belonging to a Person—the Person of Jesus Christ. It is about one-on-one face time with the Master. That was the message to the church at Ephesus in Revelation 2:4: "But I have *this* against you, that you have left your first love." He longs for us to daily share a loving relationship with Him and not be bothered by so many things but focused on Him first. He longs to be our first love.

PARADISE LOST

The first two people in the universe were driven from the Garden of Eden because of their sin. Their eyes opened to know they were naked, and now they were ashamed of it. No longer did they walk in the coolness of the Garden with God with nothing in between them. They never walked in this Garden again, as they were forever banished from it. This beautiful, hand-sculpted place made for Adam and Eve became off-limits to them. How awful!

But even more awful than all of this is that we never read of them having the same kind of intimate relationship with the Father again. Sin entered the world and became a barrier between mankind and God. They now required a blood sacrifice to provide a covering for their nakedness, which represented their sin. An innocent animal, one they had named and nurtured and loved, was sacrificed to provide a covering for them. It was a covering that kept them from being free from anything standing between them and their God. They lost everything the moment they took a single bite of the forbidden fruit of the tree of the knowledge of good and evil. The relationship they had previously had with their Creator was forever changed. Shame and regret entered their lives at what they had done. These two things were foreign to them as they had never been ashamed before nor had they ever experienced regret before. Prior to eating the fruit, they had no concept of evil. Life as they knew it was changed forever—for them and for all of mankind—by one simple act of disobedience. There is a lesson to be learned in this for us, too. No wonder Jesus despised shame (Heb. 12:2)! Shame separated us from Him.

Prior to them eating the forbidden fruit, there is no record of Adam and Eve ever questioning anything to God. They accepted what they had been told. They didn't think to eat of the forbidden fruit on their own. They trusted and believed God. They took Him at face value. Once sin entered the world, they lost that unadulterated trust in Him. When Satan tempted Eve, he caused her to doubt in God's goodness and His provision for them. She must have believed God had denied them something good; or she wouldn't have taken hold of the fruit, plucked it, and eaten it.

Satan still likes to sow seeds of doubt in people. We see this type of doubt and lack of believing in God's goodness still in our world today. When bad things happen, questions are raised about God's goodness and even His existence. The question heard time and time again is "If God really exists, how can a good God let bad things happen?" This is the ultimate question Satan wanted planted in the minds of all people when he enticed Eve to eat the fruit. He sowed doubt in the world with his original question to Eve. *Does God exist? If He exists and doesn't stop evil, how can He be good? Wouldn't you like to be like Him?* And on and on the questions and doubts go.

A LOSS OF EPIC PROPORTIONS

"So He drove the man out; and at the east of the garden of Eden He stationed the cherubim and the flaming sword which turned every direction to guard the way to the tree of life" (Gen. 3:24).

Their loss was epic, enough to crush the spirit of a man, but added to that became the curse they fell under as a result of their sin, a curse we are still under today.

Did you ever stop to think about the fact that there was no pain on earth prior to Eve's sin? We read of none, but now God speaks the curse over the mother of all the future offspring that in bringing forth offspring, her pain would be greatly multiplied. If she hadn't sinned, babies would have easily slid out of the birth canal; and as someone who birthed three children, that would have been a great blessing.

I made the mistake with my third child to deliver her naturally. I reasoned that most of the pain was over before you got to the delivery room anyway. This was long before women had the option to have an epidural to help them through the birthing process. Our only option was a spinal, right before delivery, which left me with spinal headaches afterward. Was I ever wrong in making that decision. The pain was so intense, it felt like someone was ripping the lower half of my body apart. Recovery was a lot better, but birthing—ugh! Thank you, Eve!

It is interesting to note that the word for pain in the verse about Eve is the same word used to describe the curse Adam came under in toiling the land. It is the Hebrew word *itstsabown*, meaning "worrisomeness, labor, toil, hard work, pain, sorrow, birth pangs, being in labor."[6] This word speaks of the difficulty in bringing forth children but also in bringing forth the fruit of the land. They fell under the same curse but a different form of it for each of them. No longer would Adam and Eve be able to easily go into the Garden and pick a piece of fruit; now they would have to labor to get that fruit and the fruit of the womb. Their fruit could now be cursed with worms in it.

Have you ever picked a juicy piece of fruit and ended up finding a worm hole in it because it wasn't sprayed? What a disappointment. One time, I

---

6 *Blue Letter Bible*, s.v. "itstsabown," www.blueletterbible.org/lang/Lexicon/Lexicon.cfm?strongs=H6093&t=KJV (accessed August 1, 2019).

planted broccoli in my garden. When I picked it, the heads were so pretty and green. I washed it and put it in a little water to steam. I was waiting patiently to have my first taste of my freshly picked broccoli from my own garden. When I took the lid off of the pot, there were fat, ugly, green worms floating around on the top of the water. I was so disgusted, I threw the whole batch down the garbage disposal and never attempted to grow broccoli again because I did not want to dust it with a bug killer before I harvested it. I owe a thank you to Adam for that one.

This word for pain, *itstsabown,* is used only three times in the Old Testament—two of these times in the curses proclaimed on Adam and Eve and one time in Genesis 5:29, where the verse refers to the curse upon the ground.

Adam and Eve must have been devastated by what they had done. They were driven out of the Garden. "Driven" does not imply they went easily or of their own free will. It implies they went wailing and begging to stay. Hanging onto their beloved trees. The word "drove" comes from the Greek word *garash,* meaning "to drive out, expel, cast out, drive away, divorce, put away, thrust away, trouble, cast out."[7] That does not sound like an easy exit strategy to me. God not only drove them out, knowing they would want to return to that idyllic place, He put an angelic guard with a flaming sword before the Garden to keep them from ever returning there. This was the only home they had ever known, and now they were thrust from it for all time. There was no going back to that place of perfect peace and serenity, of walking in the Garden in the cool of the day with their Creator. It was finished! They were never served an eviction notice; they were just forcibly expelled the day they sinned, no time to pack.

I have been through a divorce, and I find it interesting that the word *divorce* is part of the meaning of *garash*. It was an emotionally painful time for me, one I don't like to think about. Being "put away," so to speak, is unbearably

---

[7] *Blue Letter Bible,* s.v., "garash," www.blueletterbible.org/lang/Lexicon/Lexicon.cfm?strongs=H1644&t=KJV (accessed August 1, 2019).

hurtful. There were days when I was not sure I was going to make it through. The separation of what God had joined together was horrific. I can imagine Adam and Eve felt even more pain than this in the separation that took place for them when they were driven out of the Garden. Remember, this also ended their intimate times of walking in the Garden with the Master Creator Himself. I am sure their pain was quite intense. It would be like someone who is banished from their beloved country never to set a foot on it again.

Did you know that Jesus not only took sin to the cross, but He also took pain to the cross? Isaiah 53:4 tells us, "Surely our griefs He Himself bore, and our sorrows He carried; Yet we ourselves esteemed Him stricken, smitten of God, and afflicted." The word for grief in this verse means "sickness," but the word for sorrow, *mak'ob,* means "pain both physical and mental."[8] When pain entered the earth through Adam's original sin, God had to make a way for it to be annihilated, so part of what Jesus did on the cross—a large part of it—was to conquer sickness and all forms of pain.

I shared with you my time of emotional pain, but there have been times of physical pain in my life as well—the worse time being when I had two frozen shoulders. Anyone who has had a torn rotator cuff or a shoulder injury of any kind can understand the level of pain I endured. At times, the simplest of movements when my shoulders were frozen took me to my knees, literally. One time, like the cartoons depict, I saw stars because the pain was so intense. Praise God, He made a way, through Jesus, for us not to live in pain. In our eternal home, yes! But we can tap into His provision for a way out of pain here on earth, too.

Adam and Eve were not the only ones to suffer when they were cast out of the Garden. The Father, Son, and Holy Spirit Who had created them in Their image and breathed Their very breath (*neshamah*)[9] into them must

---

8   *Blue Letter Bible,* s.v. "ma'kob," www.blueletterbible.org/lang/Lexicon/Lexicon.cfm?strongs=H4341&t=KJV (accessed August 1, 2019).
9   *Blue Letter Bible,* s.v. "nĕshamah," www.blueletterbible.org/lang/Lexicon/Lexicon.cfm?strongs=H5397&t=KJV (accessed August 1, 2019).

have suffered many different emotions as well. God has a soul, so He has emotions like we do. (We will address this in a later chapter.) They must have experienced disappointment, sorrow over the sin that entered the world, and sorrow over what they had to do in judging that sin. Plus, the hurt of banishing Adam and Eve from the Garden. It was to be another five generations from Adam and Eve before we are told someone again walked with God. This was Enoch. Five biblical generations were hundreds of years longer than our current generations are, so, conceivably, it could have been hundreds of years later. Eight generations later, Genesis is still talking about the curse; and by the ninth generation, God is sorry He made man and wants to destroy them as if they never existed, except for one man, who walks with God, and his family.

> Then the LORD saw that the wickedness of man was great on the earth, and that every intent of the thoughts of his heart was evil continually. The LORD was sorry that He had made man on the earth, and He was grieved in His heart. The LORD said, "I will blot out man whom I have created from the face of the land, from man to animals to creeping things and to birds of the sky; for I am sorry that I have made them." But Noah found favor in the eyes of the Lord . . . Noah was a righteous man, blameless in his time; Noah walked with God (Gen. 6:5-9).

How do we stay blameless? By walking with God.

Jesus was called a Man of sorrows, and He was acquainted with grief (Isa. 53:3) He was despised, and we did not esteem Him. He became acquainted with these two things by the single act of disobedience by Adam and Eve. *Sorrow* in this verse is the same word for *sorrow* in Isaiah 53:4, where it speaks of Him carrying our sorrows. *Acquainted* is the Greek word *yada'*, meaning "to learn to know, to find out."[10] He didn't always know sorrow or grief (sickness); He came to know them because of Adam's sin, my sin, and your sin. And isn't

---

10 *Blue Letter Bible*, s.v. "yada," www.blueletterbible.org/lang/Lexicon/Lexicon.cfm?strongs=H3045&t=KJV (accessed August 1, 2019).

it interesting that Isaiah 53:3 talks of men hiding their faces from Him? The two Hebrew words are different words but carry the same meaning: an act of hiding. Exactly what Adam and Eve did—they hid from God, but He found them anyway.

I am sure the Trinity experienced more than just disappointment and sorrow from this one act, but what a sobering thought that is. My sin produces the same emotions for them and can cause separation between them and me if I stay unrepentant. We are no different from Adam and Eve. We are all guilty.

The Kingdom Dynamics section in the Spirit-Filled Life Bible tells us this about what the earth was like before the fall of mankind:

> The original order of man's environment on Earth must be distinguished from what it became following the impact of man's fall, the curse, and the eventual deluge (Is. 45:18; Rom. 8:20; II Pet. 3:4-7). The agricultural, zoological, geological, and meteorological disharmony to which creation became subject, must not be attributed to God. The perfect will of God, as founding King of creation, is not manifest in the presence of death, disease, discord, and disaster any more than it is manifest in human sin. Our present world does not reflect the kingdom order He originally intended for man's enjoyment on Earth, nor does it reflect God's kingdom as it will ultimately be experienced on this planet. Understanding this, we should be cautious not to attribute to "God's will" or to "acts of God" those characteristics of our world that resulted from the ruin of God's original order by reason of man's fall (Gen. 1:26-28; 2:16; 17/Gen. 3:16-24).[11]

Never should we attribute to God what man caused or what came about as a result of man's sin and fall. One day, the intimacy that the Godhead wanted with His created children will be restored through the Bride of Christ. He is coming again for His Bride, a bride without spot or wrinkle. One who

---

11 Jack W. Hayford, editor, "Kingdom Dynamics: Before the Fall" in *Spirit-Filled Life Bible: NKJV* (Nashville: Thomas Nelson, 1991), 6.

has been cleansed by the blood of Jesus Christ. One who is born of the Spirit and not of the flesh. When this takes place, nothing will stand between Him and His Bride ever again. Nakedness between the two can be restored as His children will have nothing to hide any more. He wiped all sin away with His one act of dying on the cross for our sin.

CHAPTER 3

IS MY WORD

At the time of this writing, the Lord has had me on an Acts 1:8 journey since 2013. This is my life verse: "But you will receive power when the Holy Spirit has come upon you; and you shall be My witnesses both in Jerusalem, and in all Judea and Samaria, and even to the remotest part of the earth." I had already been going on mission trips on a regular basis prior to 2013, but this verse took on greater meaning to me starting that year.

In 2011 and 2012, I traveled to Israel for the first two times in my life with two different ministries. When people go to Israel for the first time, I often hear them say how it changed their lives forever. My first trip was not so great, and I didn't really care if I ever went back again; so, I did not share in the feeling of so many others that my life had been changed. But it did change; it changed in a profound way over a course of time when I traveled back again and again. Within six months of going to Israel in 2011, the Lord started asking me to go back again in 2012. When He first started speaking to me about going back the next year, I argued with Him. I didn't think He could possibly be serious. I made Him give me so many confirmations about going that it is a wonder He didn't give up on me and send someone else in my place—someone who wanted to go.

I was finally convinced when I was in the line one day at the grocery store to pay for my groceries and dumped change out of my change purse into my hand to look for the coins I wanted to give the clerk. Into my hand fell a large shekel. I had been home from Israel for at least six months at the time of this coin falling into my hand and had been in and out of my change purse countless times since then. I had not seen a shekel in my change purse before this. Not only that, but the coin had a twelve on one side with a harp of David on the other side. I am sure this doesn't mean a thing to you, but let me explain. The trip I was being asked to go on was titled 12.12.12, and the main emphasis for the trip was to worship throughout the land of Israel. So, if having the coin fall into my hand wasn't enough, I got the message loud and clear with the twelve on one side and the harp of David being on the other side. The store clerk probably wondered why I suddenly started laughing as I paid her. It was all too much. I surrendered and went on the trip. That one was more of a life-changing one for me than the first one. I grew to love Israel as a result of being a part of that trip.

Beginning in the fall of 2013, I returned to Israel seven more times over the next five years. The missions the Father had for me, along with other women, were to make key proclamations from His Word over the land of Israel. Isaiah 55:11 tells us His Word does not return void but accomplishes what it is sent forth to accomplish (my paraphrase). By making these proclamations, we were sending forth the Lord's Word to accomplish what He willed to accomplish with it.

I had also been given another verse of Scripture that was to become equally important to me. Often when I returned from these trips, I wondered what exactly we had done. Had we really accomplished anything? When you can't see the results, it is hard to imagine you did anything at all; but by faith, we had to believe we had. One day when I was raising that very question with the Father, I saw an image of a large, hammer-like mallet hitting an ancient structure. Again, I was not sure what this was representing until Jeremiah 23:29 came across my radar: "'Is not My word like fire?' declares the LORD, 'and like a hammer which shatters a rock?'" I now understood exactly what the vision of the hammer hitting the ancient structure meant. As we proclaimed His Word, we were weakening ancient strongholds over the nation of Israel.

I often had another image when I prayed into this. It was of two people with large hammers striking metal spikes. The two were working in tandem with one another; first, one would make a strike, and then the other would strike the spike. Over and over again, this would take place. It reminded me of when the rails were laid out West in the United States. The Lord showed me this represented the various teams He had going into the land doing similar things that I was doing. One team would strike, and then the next one would strike—back and forth, back and forth, over and over again. The job was getting done one team at a time.

My ministry partners and I crisscrossed the nation of Israel with our word hammers, striking the ancient demonic structures ruling over the land of Israel. The Lord was gracious to encourage us along the way when we would become discouraged, still wondering what we were actually accomplishing that was making a difference. One time, my friend and I were sitting in a small pizza place near the King David Hotel waiting on our order. The waitress brought us napkins, and on the napkins was a man running, holding a large hammer over his head, ready to strike something. As we looked around the pizza place, we noticed a round emblem with the same little man with his hammer on it. Were we on the right track? I think so!

One other time, an even bigger form of encouragement was given to us by our loving Papa. This time, we were called back to Israel to reclaim Caleb's land in the area of Hebron back to the Jewish people. Hebron had been given to Caleb as his inheritance. However, today, Hebron is in the hands of the Palestinians. It is not rightfully theirs—it belongs to the children of Israel through Caleb's bloodline. My ministry partner, Ann, whom I had taken many journeys with in the land of Israel, traveled with me to Hebron to plant a railroad spike, of all things, to proclaim this land as belonging to Israel. The spike was a prophetic picture of laying claim to the land that belonged to the children of Caleb. After touring the Tombs of the Patriarchs, sacred to both Jews and Arabs, we were able to plant the spike in a small garden on the grounds of the Tomb of the Patriarchs in Hebron. We made our proclamations of the land belonging to Israel and went on with our day. About six months later, I read an article that stated for the first time in fourteen years, Israel was again building settlements in Hebron. They were taking back the land that originally belonged to them. Wow, wow, wow! I serve a mighty God!

CHAPTER 4

ALL ROADS LEAD TO ROME

As I continued my journeys through Israel, Acts 1:8 became not just figurative but also literal to me. I would become His witness throughout Jerusalem, Judea, and Samaria. I was about to take the Word to the remotest part of the Earth and had no real understanding of what the Scripture meant when saying that.

Shortly after the Iron Curtain fell, I embarked on my first mission trip. It was to Moldova. During this trip, we were taken past sunflower-lined fields on our way to a village that no American had ever been in before. Years later, I traveled dust-laden roads in the heart of Brazil to a remote tribal village. Lining these roads were massive cones of red dirt that turned out to be hives for termites. I could see these two destinations as fitting the remotest parts of the Earth.

Later, as I began traveling to Rome, I realized that during the time period when Luke wrote the Acts 1:8 passage, the remotest part of the Earth meant Rome. The Lord began transitioning me gradually from Israel to Rome—first by going to both places in one trip and then by going to Israel and later, in the same year, to Rome. My remotest part of the Earth now became the same as Paul's, Rome being my destination. Although the Rome I knew, except for the ancient ruins, bore no resemblance to the Rome that Paul would come to know. Even though we walked the same streets, the architecture and the landscape I saw looked entirely different from the ones that Paul saw.

Again, at first, the main purpose of these missions to Rome was to do prophetic acts, such as we did in Hebron with the railroad spike, and to make proclamations at key places in the city to call the Church back to God's original intent for it. The Lord started showing me that the Church was not what He had created it to be, and He wanted it to come back to the "genesis of original intent."

What was God's original intent for the Church? According to Ephesians 2:14-19, it was for the Jew and the Gentile to become "one new man," one building, and one household. The two were to be one. When Paul wrote the letter to the Ephesians, being one household with the Gentiles was a totally foreign and even distasteful comment to the Jews.

> For He Himself is our peace, who made both *groups into* one and broke down the barrier of the dividing wall... so that in Himself He might make the two into one new man, *thus* establishing peace, and might reconcile them both in one body to God through the cross, by it having put to death the enmity... AND HE CAME AND PREACHED PEACE TO YOU WHO WERE FAR AWAY, AND PEACE TO THOSE WHO WERE NEAR... So then you are no longer strangers and aliens, but you are fellow citizens with the saints, and are of God's household.

The Jews despised the Samaritan Gentiles. They would walk days out of their way to keep from passing through Samaritan territory, and now Paul was telling them they were to become part of their households. "I don't think so!" would have been their reaction. Would the Hatfields ask the McCoys to move in with them, or would the Capulets and Montagues want their children to marry each other? According to this passage of Scripture, Jesus did so much more on the cross than just take away our sin. He broke down the dividing wall between Jew and Gentile. The Church was now to be built with the Jews and Gentiles making it up together, brick by brick, interwoven together with Jesus as the Chief Cornerstone. He was what pulled the two sections of the building together. This is an example of "never the twain shall meet." But it is what Jesus made available to the two groups. Salvation is what Jesus made available to all of us—Jews and Gentiles. Would they cooperate? Would they work together to build God's household, His Church? Could they lay down what was once odious to them and embrace this new thing Jesus made possible?

Romans 11 tells us that the Gentile believers were grafted into the original Jewish roots. God's original intent for the Church was never to take the Jewish roots out but to join the new Gentile converts to the existing Jewish faith. I once had the opportunity in Israel to explain "being grafted in" to an Orthodox Jewish man. It was quite a remarkable experience. They don't usually talk to women, let alone a *goyim*. And yet, under the blue sky over Jerusalem, looking down to the courtyard in front of the Wailing Wall, my friend and I stood talking with this Jewish gentleman about how we, as Christians, had been grafted into his Jewish roots. His name was David, and a cat—of all things—began our introduction to him. God will use anything He chooses to use at any particular moment for His purposes.

The beginning of the Church began with Jews accepting Jesus as the Messiah. The first known *ecclesia* were all Jews. They were not Christians as we know the word today, but Jews who believed in Jesus as the Messiah. They kept their Jewishness. They kept the feast days, and they kept the Sabbath on the seventh day of the week—it was not originally Sunday. They celebrated Passover, not Easter.

CONSTANTINE DERAILS THE ORIGINAL CHURCH

When Emperor Constantine came into power in A.D. 312, the Church was being dramatically persecuted. Persecution of the Church began in A.D. 64 under Nero and continued through A.D. 324 by Diocletian and Galerius with many other rulers in between. It was through Constantine that it became popular to be a Christian. No one knows the vast number of Christians who were martyred during the reign of terror that took place between A.D. 64 and A.D. 312, but Constantine helped put an end to this practice through the Edict of Milan in A.D. 313. Constantine's mother became a Christian and influenced his life in this way. However, it is unlikely he became a true follower of Jesus Christ as he continued to follow the Roman gods, especially the sun god, Sol Invictus (the Invincible Sun) or Mithras, the Persian sun god. Constantine worshiped *Christos Helios*, which means "Christ the true Sun." All the same gods—just by different names, and certainly not the one, true God.

It was in honor of the sun god that the Sabbath was changed to Sundays by Constantine. He decreed that the venerable Day of the Sun would become the Roman day of rest. As a result of this, non-Jews began celebrating a pagan day as the day of rest, hence, changing the Sabbath rest from Saturday to Sunday.

Constantine hated the Jews, so he wanted nothing Jewish left in the Church; unbeknownst to him, he was trying to put an end to what Jesus told the Church to be in Ephesians. He was sabotaging one of the foundational teachings of the Early Church. By hating the Jews and changing anything in Christianity that was remotely Jewish, he took a wrecking ball to the original foundation of the Church. But there is hope. Jesus said, "I also say to you that you are Peter, and upon this rock I will build My church; and the gates of Hades will not overpower it" (Matt. 16:18). Ultimately, nothing is going to prevail over the Church, especially not dictates of any man.

Another major change Constantine made was at the Council of Nicaea in A.D. 325 by changing the time of Passover to Easter. Easter was originally a holiday to the pagan goddess Aestarte or Diana of Ephesus in the book of Acts.

According to the historian Theodoret (393-458), Constantine wrote:

> It was, in the first place, declared improper to follow the custom of the Jews in the celebration of this holy festival, because, their hands having been stained with crime, the minds of these wretched men are necessarily blinded. By rejecting their custom,

we establish and hand down to succeeding ages one which is more reasonable. Let us, then, have nothing in common with the Jews, who are our adversaries. Let us with one accord walk therein, my much-honoured brethren, studiously avoiding all contact with that evil way. They boast that without their instructions we should be unable to commemorate the festival properly. This is the highest pitch of absurdity. For how can they entertain right views on any point who, after having compassed the death of the Lord, being out of their minds, are guided not by sound reason, but by an unrestrained passion, wherever their innate madness carries them."[12]

So, here we see a complete reversal of a law of God (Lev. 23; 1 Cor. 11:23-28). One of God's festivals was replaced by a pagan celebration. Constantine went further: To sum up in few words: By the unanimous judgment of all, it has been decided that the most holy festival of Easter should be everywhere celebrated on one and the same day, and it is not seemly that in so holy a thing there should be any division.[13]

With this decree, Passover was changed to Easter for Gentiles.

Cumont, Olcott and other scholars clearly show that December 25 was the yearly date of the annual birth of Mithra. On that date, his followers held a special celebration of the fact that the sun was beginning to rise again higher in the sky. (It was lowest at the winter solstice, December 21, and not until the twenty-fifth could its rising be clearly seen.) This birthday of the sun god was made an official holiday in the Roman Empire by Aurelian about the year 273. Here is what Williston Walker, a well-known church historian, has to say about this:

12　John Foster, "Church History: Constantine, an Emperor Who Defied God," Church of God, https://lifehopeandtruth.com/change-the-church/church-history-constantine (accessed August 1, 2019).
13　Ibid.

> "December 25 was a great pagan festival, that of Sol Invictus, which celebrated the victory of light over darkness, and the lengthening of the sun's rays at the winter solstice. This assimilation of Christ to the sun god, as Sun of Righteousness, was widespread in the fourth century and was furthered by Constantine's legislation on Sunday, which is not unrelated to the fact that the sun god was the titular divinity of his [Constantine's] family."—Williston Walker, A History of the Christian Church, third edition, page 155.[14]

There are many other ways Constantine and other Roman rulers allowed pagan gods and goddesses and these practices to creep into the Church and our sacred holidays, including how they burned incense to their sun gods. This is a short summary to help you see how things went from what God originally intended to what we have today, and it all leads back to Rome, where Constantine ruled and reigned and made major decisions affecting the Church that are still in effect today.

TO THE JEW FIRST

The Jews are the genesis of all people. God created them first. They are His chosen race and need to be honored for that one thing alone, but even more so because of what all they gave to the Christian world. Whenever I travel to Israel and have an opportunity to interact with the Jewish people there, I always thank them for what their nation gave to me in the person of Jesus Christ and in my most valued possession of my Bible—without either, I would not be who God called me to be. All of mankind was given a blueprint on how to live through the Word of God; if mankind would only follow it, our world would be such a better place to live in. I owe so much to the Jewish people. Having this conversation with them has opened up many doors to witness to them in some form or another. It has brought tears to many eyes,

---

14 "Tract 22B: The Story of Constantine—The Man Who Changed the Christian Church—Supplement to Lesson 22," Champsoftruth.com, http://www.champs-of-truth.com/lessons/tract_22b.htm (accessed August 1, 2019).

and one young man even said to me that the hairs on his arm were raised when I thanked him for his people's contribution to my life.

In his ministry, Paul was sent first to the Jewish people. If they did not receive his message, then he moved on to the Gentile nations. His writings and that of Luke in Acts indicate this very thing: "That the Christ was to suffer, *and* that by reason of *His* resurrection from the dead He would be the first to proclaim light both to the *Jewish* people and to the Gentiles" (Acts 26:23). "For I am not ashamed of the gospel, for it is the power of God for salvation to everyone who believes, to the Jew first and also to the Greek" (Rom. 1:16).

Jonathan Cahn in his *Book of Mysteries* has this to say about it:

> What the world knows as Christianity, in its original and prototypical form is a Jewish faith. But something happened in those first centuries. The more embedded and established the faith became in the mainstream of Western civilization, the more it lost its original and natural identity. What was a countercultural faith became a cultural faith, what was a radical faith became an established faith, what was a revolutionary faith became the faith of the status quo . . . and what was a Jewish faith became a non-Jewish faith. As the faith became joined to a not-Jewish Western culture . . . its Jewish disciples, messengers, and apostles began to disappear.[15]

---

15   Jonathan Cahn, *The Book of Mysteries* (Lake Mary, FL: Frontline, 2016).

CHAPTER 5

SPIRIT, SOUL, AND BODY

When we were created by the Master Artist Himself, we were created with a body, a soul, and a spirit. "And may your spirit and soul and body be preserved complete, without blame at the coming of our Lord Jesus Christ" (I Thess. 5:23). Each part of our being needs to be nourished. I am not going to go into describing the amazing way our bodies work, nor am I going to go into the best way to nourish our bodies. We know how to do that all too well. I want to focus on our spirit man and our soul in this chapter. How can we nourish these two parts of our makeup? Our bodies require nutrition that is filled with the best nutrients for us to live healthily; empty calories are of no value, except to add excess weight to our bodies. What is the best way to nourish our spirit man and our soul?

Let's start with our spirit. Zechariah 12:1 says, "*Thus* declares the LORD who stretches out the heavens, lays the foundation of the earth, and forms the spirit of man within him." This is such a poetic verse relating to creation. After the heavens and the earth were created, mankind was formed with the spirit of man formed within him. First Corinthians 2:11 speaks again of the spirit of man: "For who among men knows the *thoughts* of a man except the spirit of the man which is in him? Even so the *thoughts* of God no one knows except the Spirit of God."

When sin entered the world, it entered through the disobedience of two people, Adam and Eve, spurred on by Satan. From the beginning of time, when man and woman were first created, we see that the spirit of man is willful and sinful. There is only one way to nourish our spirit man, and that is by accepting Jesus Christ as our Lord and Savior. Any other option is no option at all. If we do not nourish our spirit man with the Spirit of God, it will still be under the power of the spirit of man. The spirit of man is willful, sinful, and selfish. It can become nourished with even worse than our own willfulness if we give into the powers of darkness and nourish it by eating at the table of Satan.

When we accept Jesus as our Lord and Savior, we gain a measure of the Holy Spirit with the promise of more to come as we seek it. Ephesians 1:13-14 tells us, "In Him . . . with the Holy Spirit of promise, who is given as a pledge of our inheritance, with a view to the redemption of *God's own possession*, to the praise of His glory." The term *pledge* is a legal term meaning "earnest."[16] It depicts money, which in large purchases is given as a pledge or down payment with the understanding that the full amount will subsequently be paid. When you buy a house, you make an earnest payment with the idea you will continue to pay the mortgage off until you owe no more. This is the same principle. The Holy Spirit is given as a down payment with the idea of a continual in-filling of the third Person of the Trinity as you desire more of Him. In my experience, it is something you must seek after for more. As disciples of the Lord, we are to be continually filled with the Holy Spirit (Acts 13:52). Yes, we are given the Holy Spirit at conversion (the down payment of Him), but we need to keep seeking the more of Him. Luke 11:13 tells us to even ask for the Holy Spirit: "If you then, being evil, know how to give good gifts to your children, how much more will your heavenly Father give the Holy Spirit to those who ask Him?"

I was raised in a mainline denominational church. I was what you call a cradle roll kid. I loved to go to church and at the age of twelve accepted Jesus

---

16 *Blue Letter Bible*, s.v. "arrabōn," www.blueletterbible.org/lang/Lexicon/Lexicon.cfm?strongs=G728&t=KJV (accessed August 1, 2019).

as my Lord and Savior. I grew in my faith for a few years and then seemed to hit a plateau where my Christian walk was just ho hum. I can remember going forward at church one Sunday when an altar call was given and crying out to my pastor that I felt like something was missing in my walk with the Lord. I wanted so much more than I was currently experiencing. He patted me on the shoulder and told me I would get over it. That was not what I wanted or needed to hear. I wanted real answers to the burning desire in my soul for more of God. This was an answer devoid of hope for more and lacking in understanding of the magnitude of what Jesus purchased for us.

The Christian music group Jesus Culture has a song, "Set A Fire," with lyrics that matched my hunger at that time: "Set a fire down in my soul/That I can't contain, I can't control/I want more of You, God/I want more of You, God."[17] I had no one to tell me where to get the more I was seeking, until . . . One day, a high school friend of mine came to my house for a visit. She and I had been friends for many years. I was praying for the persecuted Church at that time in my life and had run out of ways to pray. I asked her, "How do you pray when you don't know what to pray?" She was what some would call a Spirit-filled believer. She immediately told me about the baptism of the Holy Spirit and how it was for anyone who wanted more of God. She prayed with me that day and told me about how the Holy Spirit would give me a prayer language of my own to pray with. A language, known or unknown, to man but known to God. My life changed after that encounter with the Holy Spirit. My spirit man was full to overflowing; I could hardly contain it—like the song states.

Once we have taken Jesus as our Lord and Savior and received the Holy Spirit into us, we are now under His leading and not our own spirit's leading. He is, after all, called the Helper. He is given to us as a Helper, Guide, Teacher, Comforter, and so much more. He knows far better than I do what I need. He helps in decision-making. He stops me from sinning by putting His hand

---

17 Jesus Culture, Live from New York, Integrity Music, 1-8, 2012, compact disc.

over my mouth to keep me from saying something I don't need to say or restrains me from doing something I don't need to do. He leads me into truth and understanding of the Word of God and so much more. Whenever I am stumped by a particularly difficult passage of Scripture, I seek the Holy Spirit's help; after all, He did pen it through those He gave it to.

Proverbs 20:27 tells us, "The spirit of man is the lamp of the LORD, Searching all the innermost parts of his being." This verse almost sounds like our conscience to me. You know, that little nagging voice that tells you not to do something when you really, really want to do it. With the Holy Spirit's help, it is so much easier to listen to that Voice of reason that keeps us on the right path and our hand out of the proverbial cookie jar. The Holy Spirit will give us the necessary correction and direction we need as we seek Him for answers.

AS THE DEER PANTETH

Now, let's talk a little about our soul. It has been just recently in my life that the Lord has been teaching me a lot about our souls. There are passages of Scripture that we become so familiar with that reading them becomes as rote as singing favorite old hymns we have known our whole lives. We fail to recognize the value of them anymore. One such passage to me—and I would imagine to a lot of us—is Psalm 23, specifically the first part of verse three. I recently was reading this Psalm; and when I read verse three—"He [the Shepherd] restores my soul"—that phrase impacted me so strongly, I knew the Lord wanted to speak something to me through it.

We have been taught over the years that our soul is not necessarily a good thing. That it is the seat of our mind, will, and emotions, and yet here, the psalmist is saying the Shepherd restores our souls. Why would our souls even need to be restored? Do they get polluted? Possibly. They are polluted by the world. By wounding. By wrong thinking and teachings. By sin. I would say the answer to those questions is yes, our souls need to be restored because they are polluted. And consequently, our souls need to be restored by Jehovah-Rohi—"the Lord is my Shepherd." To restore means to return or turn back. Our souls need to be restored back to the genesis of God's original intent for them.

Let's look at the Hebrew and Greek meanings for the word *soul*. The Hebrew word *nephesh* means "soul, self, life, creature, person, appetite, mind, living being, desire, emotion, passion; that which breathes, the breathing substance or being, soul, the inner being of man; living being (with life in the blood); the man himself, self, person or individual; seat of the appetites; seat of emotions and passions; activity of mind; activity of the will; activity of the character."[18]

In comparison, the Greek word *psyche* means "breath; the breath of life; the vital force which animates the body and shows itself in breathing of animals, of men, that in which there is life; a living being, a living soul; the seat of the feelings, desires, affections, aversions (our heart, soul, etc.) the (human) soul in so far as it is constituted that by the right use of the aids offered it by God it can attain its highest end and secure eternal blessedness, the soul regarded as a moral being designed for everlasting life; the soul as an essence which differs from the body and is not dissolved by death (distinguished from other parts of the body)."[19] I particularly like the meaning of the inner being of man. It takes me back to what I just shared about the spirit of man. Our soul is our inner most being, the part of us that only God knows—our inner desires, thoughts, and emotions. And yes, at times it needs to be restored back to a place of purity.

GOD HAS A SOUL

Did you know that God has a soul? Look at I Samuel 2:35: "But I will raise up for Myself a faithful priest who will do according to what is in

---

18 *Blue Letter Bible*, s.v., "nephesh," www.blueletterbible.org/lang/Lexicon/Lexicon.cfm?strongs=H5315&t=KJV (accessed August 1, 2019).
19 *Blue Letter Bible*, s.v. "psyche," www.blueletterbible.org/lang/Lexicon/Lexicon.cfm?strongs=G5590&t=KJV (accessed August 1, 2019).

My heart and in My soul; and I will build him an enduring house, and he will walk before My anointed always." The Lord is conversing with Eli here about Eli's two sons, Hophni and Phineas, when He makes the statement about His soul.

Psalm 11:5 also speaks of the Lord's soul: "The Lord tests the righteous and the wicked, And the one who loves violence His soul hates." And again, in Matthew 12:18, "BEHOLD, MY SERVANT WHOM I HAVE CHOSEN; MY BELOVED IN WHOM MY SOUL IS WELL-PLEASED; I WILL PUT MY SPIRIT UPON HIM, AND HE SHALL PROCLAIM JUSTICE TO THE GENTILES." This is the Father speaking of His soul being pleased with His Son.

Jesus' soul was grieved before His death. Matthew 26:38 says, "Then He said to them, 'My soul is deeply grieved, to the point of death; remain here and keep watch with Me.'" There are many more passages that mention the soul of God or of Jesus, but these give you an idea of what I am talking about.

If God has a soul, how can our souls be a bad thing, since we were created in His image? They can only be bad if we let them be by allowing the things of self and the world to creep in and push out the things of God. That is why our souls need to be restored periodically. How do we do that? By faith—just make the same faith statement the psalmist did and proclaim the Shepherd, Jehovah-Rohi, restores your soul. Speak it forth with the authority we have been given in the Word of God to proclaim and declare and then repent where repentance is needed and get back into a right relationship with the Lord.

Let's look at some more passages of Scripture regarding our souls. In one passage, the Lord is telling the Israelites to keep His commandments, and He says, "This day the LORD your God commands you to do these statutes and ordinances. You shall therefore be careful to do them with all your heart and with all your soul" (Deut. 26:16). "Do them with . . . all your soul"—do them with your whole being.

A similar passage is in Deuteronomy 30:2, 6: "And you return to the LORD your God and obey Him with all your heart and soul according to all that I command you today . . . Moreover the LORD your God will circumcise your heart and the heart of your descendants, to love the LORD your God with all your heart and with all your soul, so that you may live." Verse ten in this same chapter says a similar thing. Notice how heart and soul are always together in these passages, even when God is speaking of Himself. If our soul is in a right relationship with God, then our heart will be, too.

According to Psalm 25:12-13, if we fear the Lord, our soul will abide in prosperity, and the Lord will instruct us, among other blessings: "Who is the man who fears the LORD? He will instruct him in the way he should choose. His soul will abide in prosperity, And his descendants will inherit the land."

Below are some key verses on our souls. I have highlighted the key words related to our souls in each passage. Meditate on the importance of each of these words about our souls (emphasis mine):

- "Only give heed to yourself and **keep your soul diligently**, so that you do not forget the things which your eyes have seen and they do not depart from your heart all the days of your life; but make them known to your sons and your grandsons" (Deut. 4:9).
- "While another dies with a **bitter** soul, never even tasting *anything good*" (Job 21:25).
- "**Guard** my soul and deliver me; do not let me be ashamed, for I take refuge in You" (Psalm 25:20).
- "Why are you in **despair**, O my soul? And why are you **disturbed** within me? **Hope** in God, for I shall again praise Him, the help of my countenance and my God" (Psalm 43:5).
- "On the day I called, You answered me; You made me bold with **strength** in my soul" (Psalm 138:3).
- "Bring my soul **out of prison**, so that I may give thanks to Your name . . . " (Psalm 142:7).

- "For **the enemy has persecuted** my soul; he has crushed my life to the ground; he has made me dwell in dark places, like those who have long been dead" (Psalm 143:3).
- "A fool's mouth is his ruin, and his **lips are the snare** of his soul" (Prov. 18:7).
- "Does the Lord take delight in thousands of rams, in ten thousand rivers of oil? Shall I present my firstborn *for* my rebellious acts, the fruit of my body for the **sin** of my soul" (Micah 6:7).

These are just a few biblical passages about the soul. There are many more that are worth exploring, but you can see by these verses that there are many things that can happen—both good and bad—to our souls; that is why they need to be restored periodically.

My father was a mechanic who owned his own service station back in the day when gas stations also offered repair services, unlike the offerings of gas stations today, where you can buy anything from T-shirts to donuts and coffee. Any mechanic will tell you that you must change the oil in your vehicle according to the recommendations of the manufacturer to keep it running smoothly and lasting longer. Just as a car's oil gets polluted, our souls can be polluted. We must "change the oil" in our souls, so to speak, by allowing our heavenly Mechanic, Jesus, to restore our souls. Let Him search your heart and soul and, as David prayed, find if there is any hurtful way in you. Then if there is, let it be cleansed by the power of the Holy Spirit to keep yourself running smoothly.

CHAPTER 6

IN OUR IMAGE

When Adam was created by the Godhead, he was created in the image of the Trinity. Genesis 1:26 says, "Then God said, Let Us make man in Our image, according to Our likeness." Notice it says, "in Our image." This was not singular but plural—in the image of each Person of the Godhead—the Father, the Son, and the Holy Spirit. What exactly does this mean to us that we are created in the image of each Person of the Trinity? The word *image* means "in His likeness." So, we were created to be like God. That is only possible if we are born again. Prior to being born again, we cannot be like God in any way. Once we receive Jesus as our Savior and receive the Holy Spirit as a down payment in our life, then we can be changed into His image from glory to glory.

Originally, man was to be fruitful, to replenish the earth; and as he multiplied, he was creating others like himself, made in the image of God. God wanted a lot more people like this man and woman He had just created. He made the originals; now, it was up to them to create more of the same. If they were to rule the earth, then it would take more than the first two people God created to do this. When Adam was created, God said it was very good. He wanted more very good people to walk with in the Garden in the cool of the day, so He told them to multiply.

Adam was given the task of subduing and ruling the earth and all that was in it. God gave Adam a purpose for living as soon as he was created—subdue and rule. Men and women need a purpose for living; or they give up, and life is not worth living.

My grandfather was forced to retire at seventy-three years of age. Prior to retirement, he was healthy and had a reason to get out of bed each day. There was nothing physically wrong with him to keep him from doing his job; but the company made a new policy about retirement age, and he exceeded that age. From the day he retired, he sat down and did nothing but twiddle his thumbs—first one way and then the other way, back and forth. This went on all day long. Within six months of his retirement, he was dead. In his mind, he no longer had a purpose to live.

Adam was placed in the Garden to cultivate and take care of it. He had the privilege of naming all the beasts of the field and every bird of the sky. That would have been a big undertaking to name all of those creatures. It must have taken some time. During that time, God realized Adam had no one with whom to share his life. So, God created Eve.

Before Eve came into existence, Adam was told not to eat of the fruit of the tree of knowledge of good and evil. I wonder what would have happened if Adam had not taken the fruit Eve handed him and eaten it. She had already partaken of it; so, if Adam turned it down, would his refusal have saved them being cast out of the Garden? It is a good question but one we will never have an answer to.

In the next chapter, we are going to look at God's original intent for women. But in this chapter, I would like to look at what God's original intent for men was. For that, I would like to start in Ephesians 5:25-32:

> Husbands, love your wives, just as Christ also loved the church and gave Himself up for her, so that He might sanctify her, having cleansed her by the washing of water with the word, that He might present to Himself the church in all her glory, having no spot or wrinkle or any such thing; but that she would be holy and blameless. So husbands ought also to love their own wives as their own bodies. He who loves his own wife loves

himself; for no one ever hated his own flesh, but nourishes and cherishes it, just as Christ also *does* the church, because we are members of His body. FOR THIS REASON A MAN SHALL LEAVE HIS FATHER AND MOTHER AND SHALL BE JOINED TO HIS WIFE, AND THE TWO SHALL BECOME ONE FLESH. This mystery is great; but I am speaking with reference to Christ and the church.

From this New Testament passage, we can glean more about a man's role in navigating life. We have already seen that it was not good for him to be alone, so he was given a wife to be by his side. Now Paul tells us how this wife is to be treated by her husband. I find it interesting that Adam was not told this in the beginning when woman was first created. Probably because there was no sin yet, it was not necessary to tell Adam how to treat his wife. He would automatically treat her the way God would want him to. After all, he was created in God's image, and God would only want the best for her and would love her as she should be loved. Hundreds of years later, after sin and death had entered the once-pristine world, it was necessary to teach the people how to love their wives. They now had a real-time example of this through the person of Jesus Christ, as we see from the passage of Scripture we just read.

How did Christ love the Church? He laid down His life for her. There may be times when husbands are called upon to protect their wives in such a way that it costs them their lives, and Christ shows they need to be willing to do this. But metaphorically, it could mean laying down their personal agendas and listening to the Lord's voice that sometimes comes through their wife's wisdom.

Husbands are to help their wives be the best that they can be. Human men cannot make their wives holy, but they can help them along this path to becoming holy themselves through the Lord Jesus Christ. They can encourage them to pray, read their Bibles, attend a Bible study, join a prayer group, or provide the means for them to attend conferences that will help them to grow into women who are holy and blameless. They can study the Bible together and pray together with the men taking on the role of priest in their homes and making this a priority. They should not antagonize their wives or argue with them over menial things that are of no earthly purpose. We see in the Ephesians 5:25-32 passage we just read that Jesus sets the Church apart and sanctifies her. This is just another term for making her holy. A husband can set his wife apart by loving her over all people and other things, including work and sports. He can set her apart by esteeming her for the woman that she is and letting her know this and not looking longingly at another woman.

Another passage says that husbands are to honor their wives, so their "prayers will not be hindered" (1 Peter 3:7). Men, are your prayers hindered? Maybe you need to check and see if you are honoring your wife or tearing her down or putting her in uncomfortable situations?

You have been given a precious gift in a wife, and she needs to be treated as such. Christ loves the Church unconditionally. Do you put conditions on your love for your wife? What if she no longer has the girly figure she had when you first married her? Will your eye stray to women who still have nice figures?

I saw an example of Christ's love for the Church through a couple I knew one time that was so precious. I will call them Phil and Connie. They went on a mission trip to Asia, and while there, the wife had a massive stroke. They were able to save her life and bring her back to the States for treatment. However, the stroke was so devastating that she was never the same after that. She could not bring forth the words that she so desperately wanted to bring from her head to go out of her mouth. If they came out at all, they were garbled and hard—if not impossible—to understand. She had a hard time eating and could no longer walk and was in a wheelchair. Consequently, she gained weight and no longer looked like the wife he left the States with before the trip to Asia.

They had been close to my mother before she died. Connie especially loved my mother. Phil even took part in my mother's funeral. At the time of the viewing the night before the funeral, I had an opportunity to spend a little time with this lovely couple. I had heard a lot about them through my mother and had met them many years before but didn't really know them, just about them. Connie wanted to tell me how much my mother meant to her. She struggled and tried so hard to get the words out but could only do it with Phil's help. Phil had learned her new language and could often tell what she was trying to say. He stood to her side, and there was such a look of love on his face for his wife, the likes of which I have never seen. He absolutely adored her, even with the limitations and disabilities she now had. She was his wife, and he was just happy to have her alive in any form. That is the best picture I know to show how Christ loves His Church.

We all have our limitations, disabilities, sin nature, and ugliness at times when we treat people wrongly, but Jesus stands back and says, "That is My bride. Isn't she beautiful?" He knows the thoughts of our hearts and can interpret our motives, but He still loves us. He knows we are a work in progress, and He is willing to be patient with us and help us to get to where He wants us to be in our walk with Him. It doesn't matter to Him what we look like or how easily things come to us. He just loves us no matter what.

More than ten years later, Phil still looks at Connie the same way he did that long-ago evening at the funeral home when she was trying to talk with me about my mom. His love for her hasn't faded after all these years of dealing with her disabilities. It hasn't been easy for him either. They had to move out of state to be closer to their children. He must contend with the logistics of getting her in and out of the car and then in and out of places in her wheelchair. I am sure he must have to bathe her and do most things for her, but his love for her continues and is strong toward her. He stands by her side and looks adoringly at her today just as he did all those years ago. That is how Christ is with us. He loves us! Do you get that? He loves you! No matter what state you are in, He loves you!

Husbands, if you love you wives in this way, there is not a woman on this planet who will not respond to that kind of love in a positive and loving way herself.

I met a French nun in Abu Gosh, Israel, several years ago. She had given up everything to serve the church. She was elderly, so she had been serving the church for many years. There was another older nun with her, and we asked if we could pray for them. As I prayed for the French nun, I saw a picture of the Father holding her on his lap and loving on her. I just sensed the Lord had such a great love for her. When I shared with her how much the Lord loved her, she said something quite shocking to me. She kept repeating over and over, "I never knew; oh my, I never knew." Here is a woman who had dedicated her life to serving the Lord and never knew He loved her. Please, reader, don't be one who goes through life not knowing how much the Lord loves you. He doesn't care what you look like, how much money you make, how many ways you serve Him; He just loves you. We have come full circle back to the Garden, where He wants to have a personal, intimate loving relationship with you in every aspect of your life. He loves you as you are; and while He wants you to grow up in Him in all aspects, He will continue to love you no matter what.

Men, love your wives the same way Christ loves the Church. Provide for them as the Lord does for us, encourage them, pat them on the back, and look adoringly at them.

CHAPTER 7

A SUITABLE HELPER

When the Creator looked at the first man He had created, what did He see? He saw someone who needed companionship with a like creature. Adam had animals in the Garden with whom to interact; he even had God to commune with. But God saw Adam needed someone like himself to help him through life, so He created a woman to come alongside him as a companion to help him through life's difficulties and to share the joys of life.

Adam's existence would have been lonely without Eve to share the Garden. They became a team tending the Garden together. Taking care of the Garden before the Fall was not a laborious task; it would have been a pleasure. Many people—myself included—like to garden, even with the difficulties of it today, the Fall having made tending it much harder. Taking care of the Garden of Eden before Adam sinned and the Curse was put on the land would have been pure joy—joy that would have only been enhanced by having someone to talk to and work with while you were tending it. A project such as this would have been lonely doing it by oneself.

My earliest understanding of the phrase I was given—"genesis of original intent"—was what I felt the Lord had intended the Church to be. It wasn't until I was sitting in ancient Philippi in Greece under the most glorious azure blue sky I had ever seen that further revelation came to me about this phrase. Never in North America, where I live, have I ever seen this sky color. It was such a deep shade of blue, without looking stormy, and the clouds that day were so puffy and white that I could hardly quit looking at the sky. In the forefront of this spectacular sky were mountains and ancient ruins all around. The scene was beyond description.

Further revelation to this phrase came as I was sitting beside a quiet, lazy stream in Philippi called "Lydia's Spring." It was named after Lydia in the Bible, who was the first convert of Paul in Philippi—the one who was a seller of purple. We were told that historically, this stream was where she was baptized. We were also told that the women in that time period met at the spring to pray. I can't say that anyone told me they had no other option but to meet there to pray, where the men weren't, but that was the assumption I made. I later learned through some research that even the men met at a river nearby to pray and worship because there was no formal synagogue in that area. But when I first thought that the women were not able to meet anywhere else, it made me slightly angry.

In some denominations, women are relegated to places behind the men. They are permitted to teach children or other women, but not men. They can prepare meals and clean but are not called upon to serve in more prominent capacities, such as being deacons or elders. I have seen it with my own eyes many times. First Timothy 2:12 says that women are not to teach men, but I think this was a historical reference to what was happening in that particular church during that time period. I feel this way because Paul also said that if we are baptized in Christ, we are all the same: "There is neither Jew nor Greek, there is neither slave nor free man, there is neither male nor female; for you are all one in Christ Jesus" (Gal. 3:28).

So, I began asking myself after that serene day by Lydia's Spring, "What was God's original intent for women?" Let's look at some examples to see. In 1 Timothy 5:9-10, there is a list of qualities that make up a godly woman—in this instance, a widow. My paraphrase of those qualities are: the wife of one man, having a reputation for good works, the mother of children, hospitable, humble, and helpful. This does not mean women who have had more than one husband or who have not raised children are not women whom God can use. On the contrary, sometimes the more "stuff" we have been through qualifies us to help more people through their similar "stuff."

First Peter 3:2-4 mentions the qualities of a woman that are pleasing to God: "As they observe your chaste and respectful behavior. Your adornment must not be *merely* external—braiding the hair, and wearing gold jewelry, or putting on dresses; but *let it be* the hidden person of the heart, with the imperishable quality of a gentle and quiet spirit, which is precious in the sight of God." And speaking of both men and women, 1 Peter 3:8-9 says, "To sum up, all of you be harmonious, sympathetic, brotherly, kindhearted, and humble in spirit; not returning evil for evil or insult for insult, but giving a blessing instead; for you were called for the very purpose that you might inherit a blessing."

The Proverbs 31 woman has similar qualities with a few more added to it. She is all of the above; plus, she is an excellent wife, works with her hands, takes care of all the buying and cooking of food for her family, is an entrepreneur who buys and sells and makes money at it. She is strong; helps the needy; makes sure her family is clothed; and is wise, trustworthy, valiant, and not idle. Most of all, she fears the Lord.

Comparing these women to Eve, the first woman, the genesis of women is not going to be like comparing apples to apples. There were not yet other people on the planet to help, so Eve could not take care of the needy, be hospitable, or devote herself to good works (except tending to the animals, Adam, and the Garden). Nor could she hold down a job and make money for her household. None of those things existed yet—only God, Adam, the Garden, the animals, and herself. So just what was the original plan of God when He created women?

Genesis 2:18 tells us the main reason was to make a helper suitable for Adam. Woman was a counterpart to man. In the Hebrew text, the word "helper" or "helpmeet" is *ezer*, which means "one who helps or succour."[20] I

---

20 *Blue Letter Bible*, s.v. "ezer," www.blueletterbible.org/lang/Lexicon/Lexicon.cfm?strongs=H5828&t=KJV (accessed October 1, 2019).

have to confess, I did not know what the word *succour* meant, so I had to look it up. As a noun, it means "assistance and support in times of hardship or distress"; as a verb, it means "to give assistance or aid to."[21] Seeing the meaning of *succour* helped me to understand the role of Eve more than just saying she was to be a helpmeet. That is important, but help can be in many forms. *Succour* carries a different connotation to it.

I think we can all agree that God is all-knowing. He is omniscient. One definition of omniscience is that He encompasses all knowledge of the universe past, present, and future. Keeping that in mind, He had to have known Adam and Eve would sin, and hardship would come into the world through their sin, thereby causing Adam to need a helper through times of hardship and lonely days.

Besides the visible physical differences between men and women, there is one thing a woman has that a man does not have—a womb. Had women not been created with a womb, Mary could never have carried the Messiah within her body; actually, no other person could have ever been born. Only Adam and Eve would have existed unless God continued to create man from dust and woman from man's side. God created woman with a womb from the very beginning. Eve didn't just receive her womb after she sinned so that she would have pain in childbirth; she had a womb from the onset of having life breathed into her. Because of God's sovereignty in knowing mankind would sin, He not only made a way for us to be redeemed back to Himself through Jesus Christ, but He also made a carrier for His Son to be born of a woman. Symbolically, whether male or a female, if you are a Christian, you carry Christ within you to see that He is birthed through you to other people.

Solomon tells us in Ecclesiastes:

> Two are better than one because they have a good return for their labor. For if either of them falls, the one will lift up his companion.

---

21 Bing.com, *s.v.*, "succour," www.bing.com/search?q=succour+definition&form (accessed October 1, 2019).

But woe to the one who falls when there is not another to lift him up. Furthermore, if two lie down together, they keep warm, but how can one be warm *alone*? And if one can overpower him who is alone, two can resist him" (Eccl. 4:9-12).

Solomon knew the importance of having a partner alongside you to help in times of trouble.

On my missions, I usually travel with one other woman—or occasionally with more people—or I meet up with people on the ground where I am. Let me tell you, there is nothing lonelier than being in a foreign country by yourself. One time, the Lord asked me to go into Israel and Jordan and to the Egyptian border by myself. He would not let another human being go with me, even though I sought people to go. He shut the door tightly to anyone even thinking about going with me. That was the longest, loneliest trip I have ever taken.

From the moment I got off the plane, went through all the checkpoints at the airport, and got on the sherut, a local transport, to take me to Jerusalem and then back to the airport eleven days later, I was alone. Those days were endlessly long. I ate alone. I walked the streets of Eliat alone, where I stayed for a few days near the Egyptian border and my jumping off point into Jordan. I spent many days in Jerusalem alone, and none of it was fun. At times, it tried my stamina and emotions to the limit.

On the other hand, the contrast to this is traveling with someone else with whom you can experience things together. You laugh together, eat together, pray together, and, at times, cry together. You may even make an evening run across Rome by bus to get a piece of the world's best cheesecake ever. This is not something I would do alone. It can also be walking ancient paths in the heart of Israel with someone else and experiencing the Lord's presence together. These paths are not tourist destination sites, just ones you stumble divinely across to experience God in an unknown, out-of-the-way place in the land where His Son dwelled for a time. All of it is made better because you are sharing it with someone. They give you courage to do things and go places you wouldn't attempt alone. These women—my sisterhood—and I have memories of places and experiences that I have with no other human being on the planet, not even my family members. The things we did together and the memories we share in these missions are, as the commercial says, "priceless."

I would much rather navigate through life with another person than on my own. God knew this when He created Adam, so He created a counterpart to him in the person of Eve to be his helpmeet. She wasn't created to be his servant but to work in tandem with him together, side by side. Man and woman were created to keep each other warm at night, to lift the other one up when they fall down—both naturally and metaphorically—to have each other's backs, so to speak, and of course, to enjoy one another and have little Adams and Eves together to continue on after they are gone. Eve's original purpose was to be that person to Adam.

Over time, did more evolve for women to be and to do? Yes! Hopefully, most women will rise to be the type of women mentioned in I Timothy, I Peter, and Proverbs 31. Women, you are valued and loved by the Father, and you have a role to fulfill in life given to you by the Creator. Rise to the occasion, be all that you were created to be, and remember, most of all, to fear the Lord.

A JEWISH VIEWPOINT

I love having the Scriptures translated from a Jewish perspective. They give a clearer picture to the accuracy of what the original text meant. I am including a short article here from a scholar of Hebrew and Jewish studies that was written concerning the creation of Eve. It is worth reading. *Did Eve Come from Adam's Rib?* was written by Dr. Nicholas J. Schaser.

> Most English translations of Genesis 2:21-22 read, "The Lord God caused a deep sleep to fall upon the man, and while he slept

took one of his ribs and closed up flesh in its place. And the rib that the Lord God took from the man he built into a woman."

The description of the woman made from the man's "rib" has led to the mistaken conclusion that women are inferior to men because they originate from one small part of the male anatomy. Yet the Hebrew word ____ (tsela) does not mean "rib," but rather "side." According to Exodus, for example, God told Moses to make four gold rings for the Ark of the Covenant, "two rings on one side (____; tsela) of it, and two rings on the other side of it" (Exod 25:12). Likewise, when God takes one tsela from the man to make the woman, Eve comes from an entire side of Adam's body, not a single rib.

Adam's own words clarify that Eve comes from one of his sides when he declares of his wife, "Finally, this is bone of my bone and flesh of my flesh!" (Gen 2:23). Had Eve, been created from the man's rib alone, Adam would only have been able to say that she was "bone of his bone." As Adam's bone and flesh, the woman is the man's "other half." When man and woman cleave to one another and return to being "one flesh" (2:24), the two equal halves of humanity are brought back together. The primordial couple in Genesis represents God's vision of equality and complementarity between the genders.[22]

---

22 Nicholas J. Schaser, "Did Eve Come from Adam's Rib?" Israel Bible Weekly, https://weekly.israelbiblecenter.com/eve-come-adams-rib/ (accessed September 27, 2019).

CHAPTER 8

FEARFULLY AND WONDERFULLY MADE

Readers, I have to be honest with you. I finished this book, and it was at the publisher waiting on the editor to edit it when the Lord started speaking to me about writing another chapter—a chapter that I balked at writing. This chapter to be exact. I know what I am about to say is controversial; however, what is God's genesis of original intent for us when we are being woven together in our mother's wombs? People have convinced themselves, or others have convinced them, that God made a mistake when He made them a man, when in reality they should have been a woman or vice versa.

What does the word of God say about this? Let's read Psalm 139:13-16 and see:

> For You formed my inward parts; You wove me in my mother's womb. I will give thanks to You, for I am fearfully and wonderfully made; Wonderful are Your works, And my soul knows it very well. My frame was not hidden from You, When I was made in secret, *And* skillfully wrought in the depths of the earth; Your eyes have seen my unformed substance; and in Your book were all written The days that were ordained *for me,* When as yet there was not one of them.

My heart is broken over what I see in the news and the various reports that I read of how our children are being manipulated by the enemy's evil agenda to change them from what God created them to be to what man is influencing them to be. I am speaking of the whole transgender issue plaguing our society today. The Bible, our plumb line for living, tells us that God made man and woman—not a surgeon, but God. He created us to be male and female. He did not make us neutral or with changeable parts like a Mr. or Mrs. Potato Head that can take on the parts of the other.

I type this chapter with tears in my eyes as I have just read an account of a young man who had a sex change operation at the age of eighteen. Less than a year later, he regrets it and states, "I feel as though I have ruined my life." He also wrote, "Now that I'm all healed from the surgeries, I regret them. The result of the bottom surgery looks like a Frankenstein hack job at best, and that got me thinking critically about myself. I had turned myself into a plastic-surgery facsimile of a woman, but I knew I still wasn't one. I became (and to an extent, still feel) deeply depressed." Another quote from the article I read is this:

> Heyer [a former transgender who received this young man's letter] points out the unpopular truth which Nathaniel learned the hard way is "a man is not a woman and can't ever become a woman, even with surgically refashioned genitals and feminizing facial surgery." . . . "The benefit of sound, effective counseling," he points out, "would have prevented this horrible mistake from happening. He will deal with it for the rest of his life."[23]

Another article I read states:

> Camille Paglia—a hard-left feminist, lesbian professor—has been mercilessly attacked for refusing to accept the claim that men who feel like women really are women. Paglia and other "gender critical" feminists think there's something essential to

---

[23] CBN News, "Teen Transgender: 'I Feel As Though I Have Ruined My Life,'" Intercessors for America, https://www.ifapray.org/blog/teen-transgender-i-feel-as-though-i-have-ruined-my-life (accessed December 3, 2019).

biological womanhood that no man can ever appropriate, claim or understand—no matter how much makeup, hormone therapy, or surgery he endures . . . As she told the Weekly Standard in 2017: "The biological truth is sex changes are impossible. Every single cell of the human body remains coded with one's birth gender for life."[24]

Paglia said this well—as this young man is now experiencing.

Here he is, a man of eighteen years of age, who could conceivably live another seventy years or more, and he will now have to live in a manufactured female body that didn't work for him from the very day he had the sex change surgery. This young man—according to Psalm 139:15—was skillfully made by the hand of God and is now ruined physically for the remaining days of his natural life by the hand of a surgeon. If he chooses to live as a male again and is ever able to marry, he still would not be able to father children or have normal sexual relations with his wife. Now, who do you think knew what was better for this young man—God or the surgeon? My vote is for God. He is perfect and never makes a mistake, so He wanted this person to be a boy, not a girl. And had this young man not given in to the pressure out there today and had the surgery, he would still be a man. With proper biblically-based counseling, he could have lived a full, long, fulfilling life as a man. I have to wonder how many more individuals there are like him, regretting the decision that they made but having no way to undo it.

Little children do not see each other in the same terms of gender as adults do. Most children, at one time or another, identify with the opposite sex in their play; and when they see a cartoon character or a super hero that they like of the opposite sex, they want to be them. They don't care if they are a boy or a girl; they just like the character and want to be like them.

---

24 John Stonestreet, "Transgenderism & The Emperor's New Clothes" Prophecy News Watch, https://www.prophecynewswatch.com/article.cfm?recent_news_id=3629 (accessed December 3, 2019).

They need time to grow and mature into the man or woman God created them to be before they, their parents, or others push them into making such a drastic lifestyle change. God formed their parts with the right kind of genitalia, and He wanted them to be who He formed them to be. We, as a society, need to step back from this issue and give these children a chance to grow into the men and women God created them to be. We need not rush to judgment that just because a little boy dresses as a little girl on occasion or a little girl wants to be a boy, they should have a sex change operation and all the hormone therapy to help them transition from one sex to the other. Most will grow out of it.

Here are some startling headlines from newspapers, from another online article, "Children on the Front Lines: 10 Terrifying Examples of LGBT Indoctrination":

1. "School board to ask 4-year-old kindergartners if they're gay, transgender" - Canada
2. "School board votes to let males who claim to be female use girls' locker room" - Illinois
3. "Parents magazine is encouraging folks to teach their young children that men can have periods too" - US
4. "6-year-olds forced to write gay 'love letters' to teach 'accepting diversity'" - England
5. "Trans activist promotes 'child-friendly' nude swim event where minors get free admission" - Canada
6. "Sprite Runs Argentina Ad Celebrating Moms Helping Children Cross-Dress" - Argentina
7. "Sweden is Paying Drag Queens Hundreds of Thousands to Read and Perform for Children" - Sweden
8. "Parent's don't know what's best for their kids, says teacher after inviting adult male entertainer to speak with school children" - Texas

9. "LGBTQ activist transforming schools admits: 'We're training school teachers to completely smash heteronormativity'" - England
10. "Dangerous 'chest binders' being marketed to 'transgender children'" - Worldwide[25]

As you can see by these headlines, the problem is worldwide in scope and dangerous to our children's health and well-being.

I certainly am no expert on this subject. I am basing this chapter strictly on what the Word of God says. That is always the plumb line I use and the one we should all use. "God created man in His own image, in the image of God He created him; male and female He created them" (Gen. 1:27). The term "created" in this passage is the Hebrew word *bara'*. It means to create, shape, or form.[26]

In Genesis 2:7, the term "form" carries the idea of molding something as a potter would. A potter uses his hands to form an item. He is involved intimately with the clay as it is spun round and round on the wheel. God formed us in the same intimate manner with His own hands, and He formed us well just as we are, male or female. God is often depicted as a potter in Scripture. A potter forms vessels out of clay, as their hands go over and over the clay to make the vessel they are working on perfect and just the way the potter wants it. We were formed out of the earth by God's hands. We are individually, uniquely, and wonderfully made by the hands of the Master Potter Himself.

Should we say to the Potter that He made us incorrectly? "You turn *things* around! Shall the potter be considered as equal with the clay, That what is made would say to its maker, 'He did not make me'; Or what is formed say to him who formed it, 'He has no understanding'" (Isa. 29:16). Is that how we are to treat the One Who formed us with His very hands? "Woe to *the one* who

---

25 PNW Staff, "Children on The Front Lines: 10 Terrifying Examples of LGBT Indoctrination," Prophecy News Watch, https://www.prophecynewswatch.com/article.cfm?recent_news_id=3622 (accessed December 1, 2019).
26 *Blue Letter Bible*, s.v. "bara'," www.blueletterbible.org/lang/Lexicon/Lexicon.cfm?strongs=H1254&t=KJV (accessed December 1, 2019).

quarrels with his Maker—An earthenware vessel among the vessels of earth! Will the clay say to the potter, 'What are you doing?' Or the thing you are making *say*, 'He has no hands'" (Isa. 45:9). We all question God at times about situations in our lives and things we see in the world; but clearly, as stated in these verses, we have no right to question Him in the making of us, male or female. But in submission, we should say as Isaiah did, "But now, O LORD, You are our Father, We are the clay, and You our potter; And all of us are the work of Your hand" (Isa. 64:8).

Children need to have time to grow up and mature and learn the ways of God before having man's agenda pushed on them to be something God did not create them to be. I read a lot of articles about gender trying to prepare to write this chapter but found they were all man's opinions, and it just confused the issue as each person has a different opinion on the matter. However, most agreed that gender is influenced by culture. The climate in our culture today is to ignore what God says about us and to take matters into our own hands. God's opinion on gender never changes, and His ways are always right.

CHAPTER 9

ANOTHER BEGINNING

Approximately four thousand years after the first "in the beginning" time period took place, the second "in the beginning" phrase was spoken—this time about Jesus and not creation. "In the beginning was the Word, and the Word was with God, and the Word was God. He was in the beginning with God" (John 1:1-2). Both events are epic in proportion. Without man being created and then falling into the sin of disobedience, there would have been no need for the advent of the Word becoming flesh. "And the Word became flesh, and dwelt among us, and we saw His glory, glory as of the only begotten from the Father, full of grace and truth" (John 1:14). It is interesting to note that Jesus, as the Word, was an integral part of both "in the beginning" events; neither would have taken place without His involvement.

"He (Jesus) was in the world, and the world was made through Him . . ." (John 1:10). We see from this verse that Jesus had a big part in the creation of the world and everything in it. Genesis 1:26 tells us that all three Persons of the Trinity were together at the time of creation: "Then God said, 'Let Us make man in Our image, according to Our likeness."

Genesis 1:27 tells us we were created in the image of God: "God created man in His own image, in the image of God He created him." God is a Spirit, so we were created with a spirit as part of our being, which we previously talked about. I discuss this in greater length in my book *Out of Egypt: Into Your Inheritance*. In this book, I devote a chapter to spiritual DNA—how we are given the DNA of our spiritual ancestry just as we have been given our literal DNA from our parents. We have the same spiritual DNA of our spiritual ancestry if we are born again by the Spirit of God. John 1:12 tells us that if we receive Him, we become children of God. Do not all children have the DNA of their parents? It is no different for those of us who are born of the Spirit—we have the DNA of our spiritual parents. If we are born of the will of God, then we have His DNA coursing through our spiritual man. John also tell us, "For of His fullness we have all received" (John 1:16). That pretty much says it all—we have received His fullness—all that He was, is, and forever more will be, we have living in us, in the Person of Jesus Christ.

On the other hand, Jesus had to become like us when He came to earth in order for Him to fulfill all His role encompassed. "Therefore, He had to be made like His brethren in all things, so that He might become a merciful and faithful high priest in things pertaining to God, to make propitiation for the sins of the people. For since He Himself was tempted in that which He has suffered, He is able to come to the aid of those who are tempted" (Heb. 2:17-18).

If Jesus had not come to earth in the flesh, He never would have been tempted in all things as we are. I know some of you are probably going to disagree with me, but this means He was really tempted. The account we read about His temptation in Scripture makes it sound so easy. He was tempted; He quoted a passage from the Torah; and that was it. Do you get that He really wrestled with doing what was thrown at Him by Satan? Read the passage above again. If He had not been tempted as a man in the flesh, how could He relate to our temptations and come to our aid when we are tempted?

LIGHT VS. DARKNESS

Jesus was called from the womb to fulfill the role of Light of the world to bring people out of the darkness (Isa. 49:1, 5). I can't help but wonder if verse five has a dual meaning, as so many Scripture passages do. Yes, His calling, as a man, was from Mary's womb; but from the onset of creation, He was called to be a Light to the Gentiles and Salvation to the ends of the earth (Isa. 49:6; Luke 2:32).

Have you ever entered a space devoid of light? It is an awful feeling to do so. It is disconcerting, disorienting, and even frightening to wonder what may be hovering in the dark. When I have been in these types of situations, I have not wanted to proceed beyond the first step I took into that place. It is a horrible feeling not knowing what might be there or what I might bump into or worrying about falling down by taking a step where the landscape of the place changes. Life absent of light would be horrendous. However, just one single lit match can dispel enough of the darkness to take the unknown away from the situation and make you feel more secure in that place.

We see from both accounts in Genesis and John that light and dark always coexisted together from the time of Creation. Genesis 1:2-4 says, "The earth was formless and void, and darkness was over the surface of the deep . . . Then God said, 'Let there be light'; and there was light. God saw that the light was good; and God separated the light from the darkness."

Now, let's look at the parallel account in John 1:4-5: "In Him was life, and the life was the Light of mankind. And the Light shines in the darkness, and the darkness did not comprehend it." The term for *comprehend* in this verse could have three different interpretations, according to the Word Wealth in the *Spirit-Filled Life Bible*. They are as follows (emphasis mine):

> 1.) To seize, lay hold of, overcome. Such as, v. 5 could read, "**The darkness does not gain control of it**." 2.) To perceive, attain, lay hold of with the mind: to apprehend with mental or moral effort. With this meaning the verse could be translated, "**The darkness is unreceptive and does not understand it**." 3.) To quench, extinguish, snuff out the light by stifling it. "**The darkness will never be able to eliminate it**." Light and darkness essentially are antagonistic. The Christian's joy is in knowing

that the light is not only greater than darkness but will also outlast the darkness.²⁷

The key points to this interpretation are that darkness cannot gain control of light, darkness does not understand light, and darkness can never eliminate light. Darkness can never extinguish light, but light can extinguish darkness. Darkness can never comprehend light, but light can cause people in the dark to comprehend the Light.

The term for *darkness* in the Greek is *scotia*, which means:

> Darkness, gloom, evil, sin, obscurity, night, ignorance, moral depravity. The NT especially uses the word in a metaphorical sense of ignorance of divine truth, man's sinful nature, total absence of light, and a lack of spiritual perception. Light equals happiness. *Scotia* equals unhappiness. *Scotia* as spiritual darkness basically describes everything earthly or demonic that is at enmity with God.²⁸

John 1:9-13 says:

> There was the true Light which, coming into the world, enlightens every man. He was in the world, and the world was made through Him, and the world did not know Him. He came to His own, and those who were His own did not receive Him. But as many as received Him, to them He gave the right to become children of God, *even* to those who believe in His name, who were born, not of blood nor of the will of the flesh nor of the will of man, but of God.

When Jesus came to earth as a man and was the Light of the World, the light and the darkness of the world, sin, were different from the light and darkness of creation. The first account of light and dark were in the natural realm and were a depiction of what was to come in the spiritual realm

---

27 Jack W. Hayford, editor, *Word Wealth-Jh.1:5*, s.v. "comprehend," in *Spirit-Filled Life Bible NKJV* (Nashville: Thomas Nelson, 1991), 1573.
28 Ibid, s.v. "scotia," 1599.

later after the fall of mankind. First Corinthians 15:46 tells us, "However, the spiritual is not first, but the natural; then the spiritual." That is exactly what we see happening between Genesis 1—the natural—and John 1—the spiritual. We read in Genesis 1:16-18 that God made two great lights: "God made the two great lights, the greater light to govern the day, and the lesser light to govern the night; *He made* the stars also. God placed them in the expanse of the heavens to give light on the earth, and to govern the day and the night, and to separate the light from the darkness; and God saw that it was good." God made light to govern over darkness. The government rested on Jesus' shoulders, and He came to earth to defeat darkness once and for all. The term for *govern* means "to rule and have dominion over."[29] Natural light ruled over darkness, and Jesus rules over spiritual darkness. His dominion is a dominion of light, never darkness.

Our role after becoming a Christian is to do as Ephesians 5:8-11 says: "For you were formerly darkness, but now you are Light in the Lord; walk as children of Light (for the fruit of the Light *consists* in all goodness and righteousness and truth), trying to learn what is pleasing to the Lord. Do not participate in the unfruitful deeds of darkness." Once we are children of the Light, we are no longer to be part of the darkness in the world but to be little lights—offspring of the original Light—to illuminate the places where we live and enter into and to anyone or anywhere God sends us. We are all called to be as John the Baptist was—witnesses to the Light.

MORE PARALLELS TO CREATION AND JESUS

We see these parallels again in Genesis 1:28: "God blessed them; and God said to them, 'Be fruitful and multiply, and fill the earth, and subdue it.'" It was in the natural that Adam and Eve were commissioned to rule over the earth and all that was in it; but as Christians, what are we told? We are told we have dominion over what Jesus has dominion over, as we are His

---

29 *Blue Letter Bible*, s.v. "memshalah," www.blueletterbible.org/lang/Lexicon/Lexicon.cfm?strongs=H4475&t=NASB (accessed December 1, 2019).

hands and feet here on earth and are the fullness of Him. Speaking of Jesus, Ephesians 1:21-23 states, "Far above all rule and authority and power and dominion, and every name that is named, not only in this age but also in the one to come. And He put all things in subjection under His feet, and gave Him as head over all things to the church, which is His body, the fullness of Him who fills all in all." Our dominion is a spiritual one. We are to enforce the spiritual laws of God here on earth.

The other aspect of Genesis 1:28 is to be fruitful and multiply. As Christians, we are told to be fruitful and multiply, spiritually speaking. That is our mandate. We will get into this more in the next chapter.

By choosing to come to earth as the Word made flesh and to die on the cross for our sins, Jesus brought God's original intent into being that was lost during the Fall. Colossians 1:20 states, "And by the blood of his cross, everything in heaven and earth is brought back to himself—*back to its original intent, restored to innocence again*" (TPT).

Over the years, I have, with much chagrin, heard people joke about Hell and their wanting to sit around in their underwear and drink beer and play poker with their friends there, rather than be in Heaven with the likes of Christians. I have a rude awakening for them—it will not be like that. There will be no light in Hell. It will be a place of utter darkness, for there will be no one with light in them there. It will be perpetual darkness as in the ninth plague. After Jesus' millennial reign is over and Satan is loosed for a short period of time, light and darkness will never coexist again. When life as we now know it concludes, there will be only darkness in Hell and light in Heaven. Those who are full of light will live with the Light, and those who are full of darkness will live with the dark.

"The Lamb of God who [took] away the sins of the world" (John 1:29) will be the Light of Heaven, and He will never again coexist with darkness. He won't even compete with the light of the sun or the moon; He will be the one true Light of the new earth. Speaking of the new Jerusalem, it is written in Revelation 21:22-27:

> I saw no temple in it, for the Lord God the Almighty and the Lamb are its temple. And the city has no need of the sun or of the moon to shine on it, for the glory of God has illumined it, and its lamp *is* the Lamb. The nations will walk by its light, and the kings of the earth will bring their glory into it. In the daytime (for there will be no night there) its gates will never be closed; and they will bring the glory and the honor of the nations into it; and nothing unclean, and no one who practices abomination and lying, shall ever come into it, but only those whose names are written in the Lamb's book of life.

CHAPTER 10

GOD'S INTENT FOR INDIVIDUALS

We already looked at what God's original intent was for the Church, but what was His original intent for the individuals who make up the Church? All throughout Scripture, people are called by God for a purpose. Their call is God's original intent for them personally. The term "call/called" is the Greek word *kaleo*, meaning "to invite or to summon."[30] In 1 Timothy 6:12, we are told we are called to "fight the good fight of faith" and to "lay hold of the eternal life," which we were called to confess (my paraphrase).

There are two examples in the New Testament of men of faith from the Old Testament who were called using the same term for *invite*. While there are many people who were called in the Old Testament for a specific purpose, there were only two singled out in the book of Hebrews, so we are only going to look a little at their calling.

Aaron was the first person mentioned in this way. Hebrews 5:4 says, "And no one takes the honor to himself, but *receives it* when he is called by God, even as Aaron was." This tells us that Aaron was called by God. What was God's purpose in calling Aaron? God first called Moses to deliver the people of Israel out of the bondage of the Egyptians. Moses angered God by arguing with Him about this call. Take note: that is not an advisable thing to do! Moses seemed to have a self-esteem issue, for his argument to God

---

[30] *Blue Letter Bible*, s.v. "kaleō," www.blueletterbible.org/lang/Lexicon/Lexicon.cfm?strongs=G2564&t=KJV (accessed September 1, 2019).

was that he was not an eloquent speaker and he was "slow of speech and slow of tongue" (Exod. 4:10). Even after the Lord tells Moses that He made his mouth and He would be with his mouth, Moses still asked the Lord to send the message by someone else (Exod. 4:11-13).

Do we do the same thing as Moses did and make excuses to God when He calls us to do something? We have a whole bag full of excuses; many are based on our own feelings of inadequacy and on our not trusting God to work through us or to provide the means for us to go where He calls us to go, like I did in arguing about not going back to Israel after my first trip.

After all of Moses' arguing, God chose Aaron, Moses' brother, to be the mouthpiece of this dynamic duo. The Lord then pointed out to Moses that He, the Lord, was familiar with his brother Aaron and that Aaron spoke fluently and was on his way to meet Moses. Talk about God knowing us intimately! He had Aaron pegged as a good orator and on his way to see his brother. The Lord knows our coming in and our going out. His timing is perfect.

There is nothing like having your brother or sister alongside of you to bolster your confidence. Even though the original call was to Moses, God gathered Aaron into this call to come alongside of Moses to work in tandem with him. God would speak to Moses, and Moses would speak to Aaron; and then Aaron would speak to the people. It would have been a whole lot simpler if Moses would have just agreed to do it in the first place instead of needing someone to speak for him.

I have spoken a few times when translators were needed, and it works, but it is laborious to have to wait on the translator to speak to the people in their language for you. Sometimes, the translator doesn't understand the concept you are trying to make because of cultural issues or for other reasons, and then you must stop and explain to the translator your point in another way until they get it and can tell it to the people. Like I said, it can be a laborious process. It is much easier if you can speak directly to the people and not be held up by going through another person and possibly losing your train of thought and the flow of what you are saying. But Moses was not comfortable speaking himself, so God called Aaron to be his spokesperson. What a patient and understanding Abba we have. Aaron's call was specific to him—to be God's mouthpiece to deliver the people of Israel out of Egypt through his brother Moses.

Aaron's original call expanded beyond the first job He was given. He was called to the office of a priest. He didn't start out a priest, but later, as he proved faithful to the original invitation given to him, God chose him for an even bigger role.

The next person listed in Hebrews is Abraham. Hebrews 11:8 says, "By faith Abraham, when he was called, obeyed by going out to a place which he was to receive for an inheritance; and he went out, not knowing where he was going." Abraham's whole call was huge. He was first called to leave his country, his relatives, and his father's house. He only half-obeyed this call. He left, but he took his nephew Lot with him. Lot would prove to be a problem to Abraham from time to time.

Abraham had to leave everything behind to step into his personal destiny. God had a plan to give Abraham (Abram at the time of his calling) a whole lot of land and a huge inheritance, and it wasn't going to be where he was currently living. There are times God calls us to leave people and places behind to step into more of what He intends for us. When we are asked to do that, we can't always see why, and it can make for some hard times, especially if we don't fully trust that God is in it.

In 1988, a job transfer caused my family to move from our hometown of Mansfield, Ohio, to Anderson, South Carolina. My parents, grandparents, and I had always lived in the Mansfield area. It was home. This was not an easy move for us. I did not want to leave everything I knew and loved and all my family and friends behind and move to a place that was foreign to me, where I knew no one. Looking back now, decades later, I realize I would not have entered completely into my calling if I had not moved. There were things I needed to learn in this location and people I needed to meet. There is a lesson to be learned in knowing and believing in the sovereignty of God in all situations and trusting Him for His best, even when we can't see it.

In order for Abraham to inherit the land the Lord had chosen for him, he had to leave all he knew behind to go to the place of his inheritance, just as I was asked to do. Only in this place would he receive the many promises of God for his life, including a much-wanted son. It wasn't an easy transition for him. Along the way, there was a lot of strife, much of it caused by Lot. This could have been avoided if Abraham had been one hundred percent obedient and left him behind. There is a lesson here for us, too; we must, at times, leave things and people behind to move forward into our complete inheritance and always be one hundred percent obedient.

Lot brought strife into the situation through his and Abraham's herdsmen fighting over the grazing land. He then proved to be selfish in spite of all Abraham had done for him and took the best land for himself. A little later, Abraham had to fight Lot's battle for him when Lot and all his possessions were taken. After all that, Abraham then stood as an intercessor for Sodom and Gomorrah when they were going to be destroyed. Lot was still living in Sodom at the time; this had to be of concern to Abraham. Lot choosing to live there says a little bit about his character. Where we choose to live symbolically is just as important as where our literal home is located.

What I glean about Abraham's call is two-fold. First, he had to leave everything behind to go where the Lord wanted him to live to fulfill his destiny and come into his full inheritance. Second, he was to become the father of two great nations—one of his own making, and one of the promise of God. From Genesis 18:19, we see the importance of this part of his call (emphasis mine): "For I have chosen him, **so that he may command his children and his household after him to keep the way of the LORD by doing righteousness and justice**, so that the LORD may bring upon

Abraham what He has spoken about him." This was of great importance as he was the father of us all, according to Romans 4:16. If both of his sons, Ishmael and Isaac, had kept the way of the Lord by showing righteousness and justice, we wouldn't see the conflict we have in the Middle East today. His biggest call in life was to raise righteous children. Sometimes, parents don't realize the importance of this call. It is, oftentimes, a thankless call. There are no accolades or medals that come with it. You are not on a stage receiving applause for your great oratory speech. It is, nonetheless, a huge call of God that does not need to be taken lightly.

PAUL'S CALL

One day, as Saul was walking on a road that led to Damascus, he was confronted by the Lord. He had been persecuting the Jews who became believers in their Messiah. The following passage speaks of God's call on Saul's life:

> "But get up and stand on your feet; for this purpose I have appeared to you, to appoint you a minister and a witness not only to the things which you have seen, but also to the things in which I will appear to you; rescuing you from the *Jewish* people and from the Gentiles, to whom I am sending you, to open their eyes so that they may turn from darkness to light and from the dominion of Satan to God, that they may receive forgiveness of sins and an inheritance among those who have been sanctified by faith in Me" (Acts 26:16-18).

On the road to Damascus, Saul became Paul, who was appointed as a minister and a witness to both Jew and Gentile to open their eyes to turn from darkness to light. That is the call for all of us to be His witnesses and to turn people from darkness to the light of Jesus and from the dominion of Satan to God. We don't have to have a road to Damascus experience to be called in this way; to us, it is clearly stated in the Word of God this is what we are called to do. Do you see how the Scripture compares darkness to the dominion of Satan and light to Jesus?

As Christians, we are all called to follow the commandments to love one another, to be witnesses, and to make disciples. This is not an option—we cannot opt out of following this commandment. We are also called to follow Ephesians 4:1-6:

> Walk in a manner worthy of the calling with which you have been called, with all humility and gentleness, with patience, showing tolerance for one another in love, being diligent to preserve the unity of the Spirit in the bond of peace. *There is one body and one Spirit, just as also you were called in one hope of your calling; one Lord, one faith, one baptism, one God and Father of all who is over all and through all and in all.*

We are God's letters written for others to read (2 Cor. 3:2-3). How do people read you? As one who loves or hates? As one who is patient and kind, or one who is impatient and mean? Are you forgiving, or do you hold onto grudges? I could keep going on with this, but you get the point. If you name Jesus as your Savior, then people are reading the book of your life. Are they reading God in you? I don't want people to read me in my flesh; it is not a good read. I want them to experience Jesus' love through me, as well as His other attributes.

Each of us are invited by God to do certain things He wants us to do that are above and beyond what He calls all of us to do from His Word. It is rude to say no to His invitation. It is imperative to understand what you are being asked to do and to be obedient to His invitation to the best of your ability. Just like Aaron's call changed and went into something more than the original call, so can the calls on our lives change over time and the different seasons we enter in life. As we are proven faithful in the things that the Lord asks us to do, we are then given greater responsibilities. When things change, we need to be flexible enough to change with them. The rewards will be much greater than anything we can imagine or anything we are asked to give up. Just look to the examples of Aaron and Abraham and see all they reaped as a result of their obedience in answering and fulfilling the calls on their lives.

> "But you, Israel, My servant, Jacob whom I have chosen, descendant of Abraham My friend, you whom I have taken from the ends of the earth, and called from its remotest parts and said to you, 'You are My servant, I have chosen you and not rejected you. Do not fear, for I am with you; do not anxiously look about you, for I am your God. I will strengthen you, surely I will help you, surely I will uphold you with My righteous right hand'" (Isa. 41:8-10).

Surely, the Lord will do no less for us than what He promised to Abraham's descendants. We are all children of Abraham if we have received the Lord Jesus Christ as our Savior. He will be with us, strengthen us, and "uphold us with [His] righteous right hand" just as He did the patriarchs of old.

BE FRUITFUL AND MULTIPLY

Besides becoming one new man as we previously talked about, what other purposes did God call the Church to fulfill? We are given a clear picture of part of our job at the end of the Gospel of Matthew. Jesus tells his disciples, "Go therefore and make disciples of all the nations, baptizing them in the name of the Father and the Son and the Holy Spirit, teaching them to observe all that I commanded you; and lo, I am with you always, even to the end of the age" (Matt. 28:19-20). A little broader call in the Gospel of Mark says:

> And He said to them, "Go into all the world and preach the gospel to all creation. He who has believed and has been baptized shall be saved; but he who has disbelieved shall be condemned. These signs will accompany those who have believed: in My name they will cast out demons, they will speak with new tongues; they will pick up serpents, and if they drink any deadly *poison*, it will not hurt them; they will lay hands on the sick, and they will recover" (Mark 16:15-18).

We are called to go and do, not sit and watch. Christianity is a contact sport, not a spectator one. We are not to sit in our pews week after week absorbing more knowledge. We are to take what we know—and more importantly, Who we know, the One Who resides in us—to the world. We are to allow Him to work through us in any way He chooses. Just as the remaining original disciples were given the original commission if we are true children of God, it is our commission, too.

We are also told to be fruitful and multiply. Just as the children of Israel were fruitful and became exceedingly mighty, we are to do the same as Christians. We are to multiply spiritual children, and the *ecclesia* is to become exceedingly mighty. John 15:16 says, "You did not choose Me but I chose you, and appointed you that you would go and bear fruit, and *that* your fruit would remain, so that whatever you ask of the Father in My name He may give to you." Do you see that? We have been chosen to bear fruit—fruit that remains.

What exactly is the fruit He is talking about? Galatians 5:22-23 tells us it is "love, joy, peace, patience, kindness, goodness, faithfulness, gentleness, self-control." According to 1 Corinthians 13, the greatest of all we are told to do is to love. If we are producing these qualities in our lives, we are producing fruit that remains—good fruit. The only way to do this—I speak through experience—is to let the Holy Spirit, Who resides within us, do this through us. To change us from the inside, so it is projected in how we live on the outside.

Other obvious ways we produce fruit is by making disciples of people. As we are called the Lord's disciples, when we make a new disciple for His Kingdom, we are reproducing—multiplying Him through our spiritual womb. In biblical days, to be barren carried a great stigma with it. According to Exodus 23:21 and 26, barrenness was linked to disobedience. Our disobedience to be fruitful and multiply as children of God can lead to our own barrenness for the Kingdom of God. Barren women did some desperate things to have babies, even giving their spouses to their maids to conceive for them, as in the case of Sarah and then repeated by Rachel. Leah had already had sons; but when she stopped conceiving for a time, she gave her maid to Jacob to have another child. That was some mixed-up thinking, but it was the culture at that time. Hannah wept and prayed diligently for a child and was blessed to conceive and carry Samuel, who later became a prophet called by God.

My point is this: it was so important for women to conceive in those days that they went to any means to do so. We should feel the same sense of urgency to be fruitful and multiply for the Kingdom of God as these women did to increase their households and to please their husbands. We need to reproduce after our kind. Men, women, and children born anew in the likeness of Jesus Christ. That is part of God's original intent for every Christian both past and present. If we are intimate with Jesus, reproduction will be an automatic result.

CHAPTER 11

TEMPLES OF THE LIVING GOD

As I was preparing to embark on a mission to Greece in the Summer of 2019, I was reading 1 and 2 Corinthians to see what Paul had to say to the Corinthians. When I prepare for a mission, I like to study historically and scripturally about the area I am going to be visiting. I was scheduled to fly into Athens and was wondering if I would have time for a side trip to Corinth. I tried to read the two books to the Corinthians from the mindset of those who would have received the letters at that time. Sometimes, certain passages of Scripture that we have become familiar with have a tendency to lose their meaning to us, just like the passage in Psalm 23 that we discussed earlier, where David asks the Shepherd to restore his soul. We are so used to reading it one way or hearing it preached a certain way that we skim right over it and lose the depth of what the passage is saying. When I read the following Scripture text as if I were a Greek believer receiving this letter from Paul for the first time, it took on a whole different connotation to me than it had before. "Do you not know that you are a temple of God and *that* the Spirit of God dwells in you? If any man destroys the temple of God, God will destroy him, for the temple of God is holy, and that is what you are" (1 Cor. 3:16-17).

Oftentimes, we think this verse warns us about destroying our bodies by not taking good care of them, but we don't think of the broader aspects of this verse. Certainly, it has a more in-depth meaning when God says He will destroy him if he destroys the temple of God. God is not going to destroy us if we don't take care of our bodies. We might destroy ourselves by not doing this, but God won't destroy us for that. What do you think was meant by this statement? If the temple of God is holy, do we not need to keep our temples that way? If we blatantly and willfully turn from God to a life of sin and refuse to turn back to Him, would that not be destroying the temple of God? First Corinthians 6:19-20 says, "Or do you not know that your body is a temple of the Holy Spirit who is in you, whom you have from God, and that you are not your own? For you have been bought with a price: therefore, glorify God in your body."

When Paul wrote his first letter to the Corinthians, he had preached in the Areopagus and told the Athenians about the unknown God. He had seen the temples there and in Corinth. In Corinth alone, there were at least twelve temples to various gods at that time. One of those temples included a temple to Aphrodite, the goddess of love, which fostered prostitution. He was writing to them about what they knew. What they visually saw out their windows or when they walked their streets. These were places they frequented to pray to their gods.

Their temples were all dedicated to certain deities, and all forms of vile things took place in these temples to please or appease the gods. They believed the gods inhabited these structures made of stone. Paul is now introducing a whole new concept to them. He knew that their temples housed nothing. They were empty of any god, known or unknown. They were structures built by human hands. They were beautiful structures fit for any god to live in—if they really did exist. But, of course, they didn't. These gods couldn't speak, hear, care, heal, or do anything because they were not real.

What we are seeing with Paul's letter to the Corinthians is a paradigm shift. Paul is explaining to them that when they became born again, they were now the temples of the one true, living God. They now housed the very God of the universe, the One Who created the heavens and everything on earth, as well as themselves. They were not like the empty structures all around them made of stone by man's hands. They had believed that their gods were housed in these stone and marble structures, but now, Paul is explaining to them that they are the temples that house the one true God. He is telling them they are holy because the God Who lives in them is holy, making them holy. Just as the Jewish temple in biblical days was holy unto the Lord.

One of my favorite Christian singers is Paul Wilbur, a Messianic Jew. In his song "Shema," he has a couple of lines that speak directly to God inhabiting human temples. This line of the song says, "Majesty too great to dwell/ In temples made of stone/ You have chosen hearts of flesh/ To make your glory known."[31] The word picture that these lines create is so thought-provoking. God did not want His majesty to dwell in stone structures but in warm hearts that are alive to Him.

A temple is described in Scripture by the word *heychal*, which means "an edifice, citadel, tabernacle, or sanctuary: a spacious, royal building, such as a king would possess."[32] I want you to read that meaning again and again, until the full impact of it hits you. Let it be like drinking in an ice-cold glass of water on a hot day. You are now a temple fit for a king to possess. You are a royal building, a splendid building, a sanctuary that the Lord wants to live in. *You* are all these things!

No one had better destroy these "man" temples. I am sure they had seen many temples destroyed or evidence of the temples that had been destroyed by wars or natural disasters. They had a clear picture in their minds about what the previous verses we read looked like in the natural, but they had no understanding of it the way Paul was explaining it to them. They were to glorify God in their bodies that were now temples of the one true God. This was astonishing to them. They were also beautiful structures and needed to use their bodies in a way that would glorify God, as holy buildings, not as the temple prostitutes did by defiling themselves for their false gods.

---

31 Paul Wilbur, *The Watchman*, Hosanna! Music, 6, 2005.
32 Hayford, *Word Wealth-Haggai 2:15*, s.v. "heychal," in *Spirit-Filled Life Bible NKJV* (Nashville: Thomas Nelson, 1991), 1360.

Their stone temples were made with human hands and the sweat of the backs of many thousands of slaves. These new temples Paul was talking about were birthed through the power of the Holy Spirit because of Jesus' sacrifice on the cross. "However, the Most High does not dwell in *houses* made by *human hands*" (Acts 7:48). Acts 17:24 says basically the same thing, and Acts 17:29 takes it a step further: "Being then the children of God, we ought not to think that the Divine Nature is like gold or silver or stone, an image formed by the art and thought of man." He is saying that His nature is not like that of the temples or the articles in them that were formed by man through art made of gold, silver, or stone. These new temples are the art of God built around His Divine nature in holiness. It is the Holy Spirit Who builds this new house for the Lord to dwell in, not the hands of any man. God is not a slave master.

This is also what Paul speaks of in Ephesians 2:19-22:

> "So then you are no longer strangers and aliens, but you are fellow citizens with the saints, and are of God's household, having been built on the foundation of the apostles and prophets, Christ Jesus Himself being the corner *stone*, in whom the whole building, being fitted together, is growing into a holy temple in the Lord, in whom you also are being **built together into a dwelling of God in the Spirit**" (emphasis mine).

This passage not only shows we are a holy temple but also is speaking of the Jews and Gentiles growing together into a holy temple—which we touched on in an earlier chapter.

There is a similar passage in 1 Peter 2:5: "You also, as living stones, are being built up as a spiritual house for a holy priesthood, to offer up spiritual sacrifices acceptable to God through Jesus Christ." Our bodily temples house the holy priesthood of Jesus Christ, to Whom we offer ourselves as living sacrifices.

When I made my pilgrimage to Athens and saw the great structures like the Acropolis and the Parthenon that still stand there on the top of the rocky mountain above Athens, it came to me that the magnitude of what was said to them must have seemed overwhelming. *How could I be a living temple? These buildings are so magnificent, and I am just a man. After all, these structures look out over all the city and valley below. The gods have eyes to see everywhere, and I am just a mere man who can only see so far and so much.* How mind-blowing a concept this must have been to them to believe the God of the universe would choose to make them a temple to house Himself! Realistically, if we think about it, how mind-blowing of an idea is it to us, too?

If they were at all familiar with Jewish history—which is highly likely—then they knew at one time the God of the Jews, Elohim, dwelled first in a tent and then in a temple made by hands—there was some precedence for gods dwelling in manmade structures.

PROTOTYPES FROM THE ORIGINAL JEWISH TEMPLE

What does it look like to glorify God in our bodies? Let's look at the purpose for the original biblical Jewish temple.

The temple was designed primarily for worship and was known as the house of the Lord (*hekal*). It was a place of meeting with the Lord. We are told in 1 Kings 8:11 that the glory of the Lord filled the temple. Does that not sound similar to us glorifying God in our bodies? Let's look at some passages that speak of this.

- "And the glory of the LORD came into the house by the way of the gate facing toward the east. And the Spirit lifted me up and brought me into the inner court; and behold, the glory of the LORD filled the house" (Ezek. 43:4-5).
- "So that the priests could not stand to minister because of the cloud, for the glory of the LORD filled the house of the LORD" (1 Kings 8:11).
- "Now when Solomon had finished praying, fire came down from heaven and consumed the burnt offering and the sacrifices, and the glory of the LORD filled the house. The priests could not

enter into the house of the LORD because the glory of the LORD filled the LORD's house" (2 Chron. 7:1-2).

- "Then the cloud covered the tent of meeting, and the glory of the LORD filled the tabernacle. Moses was not able to enter the tent of meeting because the cloud had settled on it, and the glory of the LORD filled the tabernacle" (Exod. 40:34-35).

We are to meet with the Lord and worship Him in the center of our being. His glory fills us. We need to live in such a way that we do not extinguish that glory by any sin in our lives but instead let that glory shine out of us in great power and majesty.

Just what is God's glory? According to Strong's Concordance, the term glory in the Hebrew is *kabad*. Part of its meaning is weighty or honorable.[33] When Moses asked to see God's glory, what did he see? In Exodus 34:6 we are told, "Then the LORD passed by in front of him and proclaimed, 'The LORD, the LORD God, compassionate and gracious, slow to anger, and abounding in lovingkindness and truth; who keeps lovingkindness for thousands, who forgives iniquity, transgression and sin." All of what this passage says the Lord is we should be carrying within us to reflect the glory of God. What passed in front of Moses was all part of His glory. You cannot separate His glory from His compassion, grace, patience, lovingkindness, and truth. The Greek word for glory is *doxa*. Part of its meaning is "magnificence, excellence, dignity, grace, majesty, a thing belonging to God, the kingly majesty which belongs to him as supreme ruler, majesty in the sense of the absolute perfection of the deity ... used in Romans 8:18, 'For I consider that the sufferings of this present time are not worthy to be compared with the glory that is to be revealed to us.'"[34] This, too, is part of God's glory that resides within us as believers.

---

33 *Strong's Hebrew Lexicon*, s.v. "kabed," www.eliyah.com/cgi-bin/strongs.cgi?file=hebrewlexicon&isindex=3513 (accessed October 1, 2019).
34 *Blue Letter Bible*, s.v. "doxa," www.blueletterbible.org/lang/Lexicon/Lexicon.cfm?strongs=G1391&t=KJV (accessed October 1, 2019).

Many times, in various situations in my life, I have felt the weightiness of God come upon me. Often, it is during times of intercession. There is no easy way to explain it, but it feels like a heaviness settling upon me or as if my hands are heavy and hard to lift. Sometimes, my hands feel huge, like Hulk hands. That is the glory of God manifesting to me.

Speaking, again, of the temple, in 2 Chronicles 6:19-20, Solomon says:

> Yet have regard to the prayer of Your servant and to his supplication, O LORD my God, to listen to the cry and to the prayer which Your servant prays before You; that Your eye may be open toward this house day and night, toward the place of which You have said that *You would* put Your name there, to listen to the prayer which Your servant shall pray toward this place.

The temple was a place where the Lord's name was put. If you are a born-again believer, all of Who He is dwells in you, along with all of what His names and attributes represent. Each of these attributes can work through you at any given time and in any given place because you are a carrier of God within your holy temple.

The temple was the symbol of God's victory over His enemies. Has the Lord not made our enemies a footstool for his feet? "The LORD says to my Lord: 'Sit at My right hand until I make Your enemies a footstool for Your feet'" (Psalm 110:1). This passage is repeated many times in the New Testament (Luke 20:43; Acts 2:35).

The temple was a place of communication, where the priests had access to the mind of God. We have the mind of Christ built within us as His temple. "FOR WHO HAS KNOWN THE MIND OF THE LORD, THAT HE WILL INSTRUCT HIM? But we have the mind of Christ" (1 Cor. 2:16). We have free access at any time of the day or night to communicate to the Lord, Who indwells us.

The temple was a place of prayer. "Even those I will bring to My holy mountain and make them joyful in My house of prayer. Their burnt offerings and their sacrifices will be acceptable on My altar; for My house will be called a house of prayer for all the peoples" (Isa. 56:7). Jesus reiterates this in Mark 11:17: "And He *began* to teach and say to them, 'Is it not written, MY HOUSE SHALL BE CALLED A HOUSE OF PRAYER FOR ALL THE NATIONS?'" As we previously read in 2 Chronicles 6:19-20, prayer is a way of communicating with the Lord. We need to do this through our spirit man with the help of the Holy Spirit—spirit-to-Spirit prayer and communication within our own person. You are to be a place of prayer.

The temple was also a place of healing.

> Then he brought me back to the door of the house; and behold, water was flowing from under the threshold of the house toward the east, for the house faced east. And the water was flowing down from under, from the right side of the house, from south of the altar . . . And by the river on its bank, on one side and on the other, will grow all *kinds of* trees for food. Their leaves will not wither and their fruit will not fail. They will bear every month because their water flows from the sanctuary, and their fruit will be for food and their leaves for healing" (Ezek. 47:1, 12).

In Revelation 22:2, we read, "In the middle of its street. On either side of the river was the tree of life, bearing twelve *kinds of* fruit, yielding its fruit every month; and the leaves of the tree were for the healing of the nations." These are symbolic pictures of the water flowing from the temple of God through the person of Jesus when He was pierced on the cross and water came from His side. Healing should automatically flow through us as the temple of the living God, as should the water of the Word.

The Holy Spirit dwelled in the Holy of Holies in the original temple, but now the Spirit of God dwells in us. "Do you not know that you are a temple of God and *that* the Spirit of God dwells in you" (1 Cor. 3:16). In the wilderness, it was called the tabernacle of testimony or witness. "Our fathers had the tabernacle of testimony in the wilderness." (Acts 7:44). The word *witness* means "testimony, proof, evidence, proclamations of personal experience, martyr."[35] In the Word Wealth in the Spirit-Filled Bible it says, "The tabernacle which evidences God's presence, is a testimony to the covenant between Him and His people."[36] When Jesus indwells our human temples and we are living our lives right before Him, we become a living, breathing, walking testimony of Who He is. We are a perpetual tabernacle of witness/testimony.

As we think about what *testimony* means, what is one of the ways we are to overcome? "And they overcame him because of the blood of the Lamb and because of the word of their testimony, and they did not love their life even when faced with death" (Rev. 12:11). We can overcome our enemies by being a walking, breathing testimony of Who He is.

Just as we are individual temples of the Lord's presence, we are also, as the body of Christ, a corporate temple.

> So then you are no longer strangers and aliens, but you are fellow citizens with the saints, and are of God's household, having been built on the foundation of the apostles and prophets, Christ Jesus Himself being the corner *stone*, in whom the whole building, being fitted together, is growing into a holy temple in the Lord, in whom you also are being built together into a dwelling of God in the Spirit" (Eph. 2:19-22).

Even though we may not personally know our brothers and sisters in the Lord around the world, we are all part of the same temple of God being built together to house His Spirit.

Jesus was our Example; He was the first living and breathing Temple, carrying the glory of God. What did He say about Himself? John 2:19 and 21 say, "Jesus answered them, 'Destroy this temple, and in three days I will raise it up.' But He was speaking of the temple of His body." This was fulfilled

---

35 Hayford, *Word Wealth-Revelation 15:5*, s.v. "marturion," in *Spirit-Filled Life Bible NKJV* (Nashville: Thomas Nelson, 1991), 1360.
36 Ibid.

when He was raised on the third day from the grave. Acts 10:40 says, "God raised Him up on the third day." Jesus is always our example in all things, including being a temple Himself, just as He has called each of us to be His temple, carrying His glory and His testimony wherever we go.

CHAPTER 12

THE BIBLE: OUR PLUMB LINE

Old time British evangelist and healer Smith Wiggelsworth once said, "The Bible is the plumb line for everything."[37] In late winter of 2019, Ann, my long-time ministry partner, told me I needed to take a plumb line to Rome with me on my upcoming fall trip of the same year. I had been sent there on mission two other times and was returning in the fall of 2019. We had both read a book by Asher Intrater titled *Alignment*. On the front of the book is a plumb line, a very distinct one. The whole cover is white with just the title of the book, the author, and the plumb line in the center. It is a very eye-catching cover. I have always liked things to be simple but slightly elegant, and this cover is both of those things. The point of the title is made when you see this plumb line as central on the cover.

I prayed about what my friend told me; and when Notre Dame burned a few days later, the Holy Spirit spoke to me that the plumb line needed to go there as well as to Rome as a prophetic act to call the Catholic church back into alignment with God's Word. While Notre Dame is being rebuilt, it needs to come into alignment with what God wants for the French Catholics. Notre Dame is to them what the Vatican is to Italy. My current ministry partner, Jasmine, and I were to take the plumb line to Notre Dame and have it

---

[37] Patricia Culbertson, Editor, *Smith Wigglesworth Devotional* (New Kensington: Whitaker House, 1999), 351.

hung while it is still under reconstruction. We were to call it back into God's alignment with the genesis of God's original intent.

I had previously had a dream that confirmed we were to go to France as well as Italy that year. God often speaks to me in dreams. In the dream, our guide who had helped us get to where we needed to be during the previous year's mission in Maoiri, Italy, was driving me and Jasmine to the border between France and Italy. I believe he represented the Holy Spirit in the dream as the Holy Spirit is our Guide. When we reached the border, I was standing with one foot in France and one foot in Italy. Our guide told me to be careful because it would be dangerous and difficult. End of dream. What we were going to Paris to do would hopefully not be dangerous, but it would be difficult to get the plumb line in the right hand to hang it from Notre Dame. This turned out to be impossible as we could not get it to a person and had to hang it ourselves as close as we could get to the cathedral. I had this dream months before Notre Dame burned. I prayed about this dream and pondered it, waiting to see the interpretation of it. As soon as the cathedral burned, the Holy Spirit put the dream, the plumb line, and the burning of the cathedral together for me; and I knew we were to take the plumb line there. On this mission, we would be in Italy and then going on to France to carry out this portion of the mission—having one foot in Italy and one foot in France in the same year.

PROPHETIC ACTS BY PROPHETS OF OLD

Often in Scripture, prophets of old were told to do strange things as prophetic acts, depicting a message the Lord wanted delivered in a visible fashion. Jeremiah was told by the Lord to buy a jar and take it to the valley of Ben-Hinnom and because of the people's great sin, give a message to them there. He was told to break the jar in sight of the men and to make a proclamation against the people and the city that God was going to break them like Jeremiah broke the jar he had with him (Jer. 19).

Another time, Jeremiah was told to buy a waistband, put it around his waist, and not put it in water. He obeyed and then was told to take the waistband from his waist and place it in a crevice of the rock at the Euphrates. A few days later, he was told to go and retrieve the waistband; but when he did, it was totally worthless. Then the Word of the Lord came to him, saying, "Thus says the LORD, 'Just so will I destroy the pride of Judah and the great pride of Jerusalem. This wicked people, who refuse to listen to My words, who walk in the stubbornness of their hearts and have gone after other gods to serve them and to bow down to them, let them be just like this waistband which is totally worthless'" (Jer. 13:9-10).

Isaiah the prophet was told in Isaiah 20:2-3 to go naked and barefoot as a prophetic act against Egypt and Cush: "At that time the LORD spoke through Isaiah the son of Amoz, saying, 'Go and loosen the sackcloth from your hips and take your shoes off your feet.' And he did so, going naked and barefoot. And the LORD said, 'Even as My servant Isaiah has gone naked and barefoot three years as a sign and token against Egypt and Cush.'"

Hosea was told to marry a prostitute, again as a prophetic act to the people of his time. There are many more such acts in Scripture, but you get the picture. I give you these because some of the things I am asked to do sound strange to most Christians, but there is a biblical precedence for them. I sure hope God is through with the naked thing! Shudder . . .

RESTORATION AND REDEMPTION

The reason for taking the plumb line to Rome and Paris was to call the Church into alignment with the "genesis of God's original intent." I went on a mission to Greece in the spring of 2019, after I had received the word about taking the plumb line to Rome. While I was in Greece, I sensed I was to buy the plumb line there, as that is where the Church in Europe first began through Paul. The Church was on God's track when it first began in

Greece; it had not yet been derailed from what God wanted it to be. It was still in plumb (alignment).

I stayed in an area in Thessaloniki where there were shops of all kinds that I walked by daily on my way to and from my ministry destinations. I kept looking for a hardware store but failed to find one. I wanted to buy the plumb line in Thessaloniki because of the symbolic meaning of it coming from where the church first entered into Europe. However, the Lord kept me blinded to all hardware stores until my second-to-last night there.

I only had one more day before I was to fly out, and that was the day that we were to go to Philippi. On my way back to my hotel that evening, I found the hardware store I had been looking for all along. I had walked by it more than once and had not seen it before. I was with another couple, and they knew what I was looking for. The man was familiar with carpentry, so he tried to explain to the store clerk, who didn't speak English, what I wanted to buy. He even drew him a picture of one, but the clerk still didn't understand what we were looking for. I happened to spot a wall with a lot of hardware items on it. We went to the wall, and the gentleman I was with spotted a plumb line almost immediately. And lo and behold, it looked quite similar to the one on the cover of Asher Intrater's book *Alignment*. I knew I was on the right track. God had confirmed His word to me.

Now if I had found this plumb line sooner, I would have taken it to the coast and missed what God really wanted to do with it. Instead, it went with me to Philippi the next day. It was among the ancient ruins of this biblical city, where Lydia lived and where Paul's work began, that we dropped the plumb bob and made declarations. I am not suggesting that there is anything supernatural about doing this; it is all according to the Lord's leading, and the results lay in His hands. But I do believe it was important for the plumb line to come from where the Church first began, where and when it was in true alignment with what God intended the Church to be. It was a symbolic picture of that very thing.

This plumb carries no magical value to it, just a prophetic picture of what God wants to say to the Catholic church in Rome and at Notre Dame, not unlike the belt Jeremiah wore and then buried. The same type of prophetic pictures that He used with Jeremiah, Isaiah, Hosea, and others in the Bible, He wanted to use with this plumb line. Please note, I am not putting myself in any kind of place with these great men of God. I am just being an obedient servant as they were. "[God] *is* the same yesterday and today and forever (Heb. 13:8); how He did things in biblical days, He will still do today. He will use anyone willing to look foolish by worldly standards and follow His leading to do these types of prophetic acts to bring about His desired results. I raised my hand and said I would volunteer to be one of those called to this type of mission, and He has taken me at my word and used me time and time again to go and do things that look foolish by worldly standards.

I now had my plumb line to take to Rome and Paris, but I had four huge hurdles to jump over before it could return to Europe with me in the fall of that same year, and be used as the prophetic act God wanted to use it for. I had to get it through four airport security checkpoints on my way back to the States. The plumb bob on the end of the line is made of steel. It probably weighs over a pound and is shaped like an upside-down pyramid, only round. It comes to a sharp point on the end and could easily be viewed as a weapon. I was traveling light on this trip due to tight connections and was not checking any bags, so it had to go through all four of the scanners on my way home and not be confiscated.

One time, I had to sneak water from Israel into the Colosseum in Rome. This was another prophetic act, a story for another book. They, too, had a scanner, and no liquids were allowed through. Jasmine, my brave travel mate, who originally had the water in her bag, handed the bottle containing water from Israel to me and said, "Here, you take it." Gee, thanks!

If you are familiar with Brother Andrew, he smuggled Bibles behind the Iron Curtain for years. He had a prayer that he prayed when he came to checkpoints on the roads: "Lord, you made blind eyes see. Now, I pray, make seeing eyes blind."[38] That became my prayer as we drew closer and closer to the scanner. I also added a prayer of my own thinking: *Lord, distract the lady doing the scanning, so my bag goes through without her seeing my water bottle.* After all, I couldn't replace this water from Israel when I was now in Rome. It had prophetic significance to it, just like the plumb line did.

As we approached the scanner, a family with a couple of children were in front of us. They had many types of liquids with them in various places in a stroller. They were pulled over to the side because of the many bottles and pouches of liquids they had in their stroller. I placed my bag with the hidden contraband on the scanner and acted innocent. Just as my bag went through the scanner, the lady manning the scanner had her attention drawn to this family in front of me, and she never looked at the image of my bag. I picked it up, walked on, and my mission partner and I went and poured the water at the place we felt led to as a prophetic act of cleansing the blood of the martyrs spilled in that place. God's purposes will not be foiled.

Back to my plumb. I had it in my bag when I went through the check-in for my first flight. It sailed right through without question. I was praying my Brother Andrew prayer again. At the next check-in for my second flight, they took it out of my bag and handed it around about four different security people to see if they would let it go through. I appealed to them that it had sentimental value to me—I should have told them it had Kingdom significance. I didn't think of that at the time. They decided to let me keep it, handed it back to me, and I went on. Two down, two to go. I decided at the next two check-in places to put it in the bin, so it wouldn't appear like I was trying to hide anything. I again prayed my Brother Andrew prayer and added one of my own for good measure.

---

[38] Brother Andrew, John Sherrill, and Elizabeth Sherrill, *God's Smuggler* (Grand Rapids: Chosen Books, 2001), 107-108.

I asked the Lord to change the properties of the metal to be like Nerf material. It sailed right through the last two screenings without anyone even looking at it. I was jubilant! It was going to go back to Europe in the fall with me to Rome and Paris as God intended.

I tell you all this to tell you how important it is for all of us to be in alignment with God's "genesis of original intent" in every area of our lives. As Smith Wiggelsworth stated, "The Bible is the plumb line for everything." What we are told by pastors, speakers, and others must line up with the Word of God. When we hear from the Lord in some manner, it must line up with the Word of God. If anyone says something that goes against what His Word says, it is not from Him. God will not ask you to do something contrary to His Word. He will let you do it, but He will not ask you to do it.

Second Samuel 22:31 states, "As for God, His way is blameless; the word of the LORD is tested." And Galatians 1:9 says, "As we have said before, so I say again now, if any man is preaching to you a gospel contrary to what you received, he is to be accursed!" That is a pretty strong statement. What they had received had come to them through Paul's preaching and writing inspired by the Holy Spirit. He did not want them to fall prey to any false teachings.

One of my favorite verses about the importance of the Word is Psalm 119:105: "Your word is a lamp to my feet and a light to my path." We can never go wrong if we align our lives with the Word of God, and it will be a light to guide us. We must align our lives with His Word as it is trustworthy and is a blueprint for how we are to navigate through the life we live here on earth. There are so many more passages in the Bible about the importance of the Word of God to us. We would do well to study them and take them to heart. God gave us our Bibles for a reason, and it is not to be a coaster on your end table or just another book on your bookshelf gathering dust. It is to be read and studied and cherished. Many people over the years have lost their lives as a result of having the Word in their homes or on their person. It is so valuable to me—one of my most prized possessions.

APPLICATION TO INDIVIDUALS FOR USING THE WORD AS OUR PLUMB LINE

How do we apply this principle to ourselves? What does the Word say about you? Not what life, your spouse, your parents, your teachers, or your peers say. But what does the Word of God say about you? The Word is the truth. The Word is what you need to align with.

Old time Western movies often depicted trains being stopped on the tracks by a fallen tree. The trees were always placed there by a gang that was out to rob the train, and the tree forced the train to stop at a place where the robbers could attack it. Our enemy, who "prowls around like a roaring lion" (1 Peter 5:8)—the one who comes "to steal and kill and destroy" (John 10:10)—does the same thing to us. He wants to stop us in our tracks and keep us from fulfilling the call on our lives by speaking something to us through words of people in authority over us. He wants to destroy our future and kill our self-esteem, thus holding us back from being all we were created to be—just like he did in the Garden with Adam and Eve. He stole the Garden from them and, more importantly, their intimate, "walk in the Garden" relationship with the Father. But the rest of that verse says that Jesus "came that they may have life, and have *it* abundantly" (John 10:10). That is His plan for our lives.

Why would the enemy do this? He is out to thwart God's plans. God has a plan and a purpose for your life, and the enemy knows this and wants to stop you by devaluing you with words spoken to you. Many of these words are spoken to us as children, and of course, we believe them. They worm their way down into our belief systems and set up a lie from the enemy that is hard to overcome. After all, parents and teachers and people in authority must know a whole lot, so it must be true.

Words are powerful. Satan knows this. They can stop us in our tracks if we let them. They deliver mortal blows to vulnerable hearts that wound for decades, even lifetimes, until they are exposed for what they are. These evil words of condemnation play over and over in our minds like a record stuck in place. It is time to break these demeaning records and listen to the music of Heaven and what it has to say about you. The symphony that flows from the heart of our Creator and our Savior says we are His beloved; we are seated with Him in heavenly places; we are the head and not the tail; we cannot be separated from His love, not even by our own sin. He has a plan for our lives, to "give [us] a future and a hope" (Jer. 29:11). These are just a few truths from Scripture about who we are. There are many more truths to be uncovered, but you will need to research your Bible to pull these truths out and then make a concentrated effort to believe them over the lies of the enemy. Let the Word of God align your thoughts to the truth, not to man's lies.

In the old movies, the trees were places upon the railroad tracks to stop the trains in order to rob them. Similarly, this is what the enemy has done to individuals with the hurtful words spoken to them. The enemy uses people to spew out vile, untrue things to rob us of our purpose in God, thus robbing the world of what God wants to do through us. Don't let him get away with it. Break the record of these endless words of destruction with the truth of God's Word. Remove the things the enemy places upon the tracks of your life to derail you from God's truth.

Align your thinking with what God says about you and not what man has said. Move the trees of lies off the track of your destiny and move forward under the power of who you are in Christ, if you belong to Him. If you don't know Jesus as your Lord and Savior, make that your priority, so all of what is said in the Word of God is for you, too. Confess your sin to Him; ask Him to live within your heart and be your Master and Savior today, and He will. Then His truths will become your truths.

CHAPTER 13

EQUIPPING CENTERS

How are disciples made? When someone is born again, do they automatically become a disciple? In one sense of the word, yes. But it takes time for them to grow into their new life to become one who is capable of reproducing and becoming someone who makes more disciples. Just as it takes a baby many years of physical growth to be able to reproduce, it takes newborn Christians time to become mature in the Lord and capable of reproducing. That is not to discount the fact that many new converts are so excited about their new relationship with Jesus that they overflow with it and are able to lead others to Christ through their witness. But they are not spiritually mature enough to train them in the ways of the Lord because they do not know those ways yet themselves.

Ephesians 4:11-16 speaks of this very thing. It tells us that we are not only to become mature men and women in the Lord but also that some will be put in positions to help equip the others to go into the world and make disciples.

> And He gave some *as* apostles, and some *as* prophets, and some *as* evangelists, and some *as* pastors and teachers, for the equipping of the saints for the work of service, to the building up of the body of Christ; until we all attain to the unity of the faith, and of the knowledge of the Son of God, to a mature man, to the measure of the stature which belongs to the fullness of Christ. As a result, we are no longer to be children, tossed here and there by waves and carried about by every wind of doctrine,

by the trickery of men, by craftiness in deceitful scheming; but speaking the truth in love, we are to grow up in all *aspects* into Him who is the head, *even* Christ, from whom the whole body, being fitted and held together by what every joint supplies, according to the proper working of each individual part, causes the growth of the body for the building up of itself in love.

This shows us that one of the original intentions for the Church was to equip the saints to do the work of service to help build the body up, to increase the Lord's household, and to make it strong.

I must ask the question, "Are our churches doing this today?" Some are, to be sure; but from what I have observed, many aren't. They are more interested in being politically correct and not offending anyone or in enticing people to come to their individual house to build up their own church and not the universal church. Churches have become program- and entertainment-oriented. I must point us back to the Garden, where it was about relationship. A one-on-one relationship with the Godhead. Are we being encouraged in our churches to have an intimate, walk-in-the-Garden-type relationship with our Creator and Redeemer? Is your church teaching you how to do this? Is it training you for the work of service to build up the body of Christ? If not, then maybe you need to look for a church that is doing these things or, better yet, challenge your church leaders to think about this and where they stand in line with the Word of God for what the church is intended to be.

When the Church first came into existence, it was a community of believers sharing meals together, teaching believers, and worshiping the Lord together. They met in homes because oftentimes, they were persecuted, so this helped to keep them under the radar of those doing the persecuting. Many of them were Gentile converts, who would never have had a place to worship before their conversion.

We saw this in our church at Philippi that met by a river because they had no synagogue in which to meet. They probably also met in houses. You will see different house churches mentioned all throughout Scripture. Until the

Gospel was taken to the Gentiles, the original church was mainly made up of Jews who came to know Yeshua as their Messiah. Some would have been kicked out of their synagogues because of their new belief in Yeshua. Their only option was to meet at a house church or at a river.

I don't see this as all bad. I have worked in several churches and different denominations for many decades, and in some ways, I think they are out of touch with what God intended the Church to be. We have large buildings to maintain and large salaries to pay. It is getting harder and harder to maintain both the buildings and the salaries, as well as the programs, because of the overhead. It would be a lot easier to still meet in small groups in homes and come together occasionally in a larger setting with other believers in the area. In one communal building, like the synagogue was. Look at the money that would be saved and could be used for the furtherance of God's Kingdom instead of paying for all that is needed to maintain large buildings.

In the area where I live, many churches have closed their doors over the last few years because they no longer had enough members to maintain their buildings and salaries. Some combined two memberships to try and stay afloat. I think our current church system is antiquated. It is my opinion we need to go back to God's original blueprint for the Church—meeting in homes in a more intimate setting. I also know that this is probably not going to happen, but we need to at least look at what Scripture laid out for us as the foundational principles of what the Church is to be.

Again, we see that Constantine had a hand in changing all the Lord intended for His Church to be.

> Yet, in spite of this mixing of Christianity and paganism in the mind of Constantine—he became the most influential determinant of Christianity for more than a thousand years! For it was through his political support that the apostate local Christian church at Rome, together with several other major city churches, grasped control of Christendom—and imposed their worldly ways upon Christians scattered in cities and villages all

over the vast Roman Empire. And the changes that took place then,[sic] have continued on down to our own time.[39]

Major cathedrals were built to worship in replacing the smaller house churches where worship and fellowship with other believers was in a more intimate and friendly setting. What Constantine did is not church; it is politics. Rituals never touch the heart of God; only true worship moves His heart.

If you look at the Beloved in the Song of Solomon, he goes to the garden to meet with "my sister, *my* bride" (Song 5:1). Then we read in Song 6:2 how the Shulamite declares her beloved has gone to his garden. Why the garden? Because that is where the love relationship between God and man began. That is where He is pointing us back to in these passages, to a love relationship with Himself. That time of walking intimately in the Garden with Him like before the Fall. He relished the relationship He had with Adam and Eve before they sinned. The one with nothing in between Him and them. He still longs for that kind of relationship with His bride today. Won't you join Him in the garden of intimacy, wherever that may be for you? He has gone to the garden to wait for you. I guarantee it will not only be a place of intimacy with Jesus but a place of beauty as well. Go back to the "genesis of God's original intent" in your relationship with Him and see what you end up birthing for His Kingdom.

---

[39] "Tract 22B: The Story of Constantine—The Man Who Changed the Christian Church—Supplement to Lesson 22," Champsoftruth.com, http://www.champs-of-truth.com/lessons/tract_22b.htm (accessed August 1, 2019).

CHAPTER 14

RESTORING AMERICA TO HER ORIGINAL ROOTS

Jesus tells us in Matthew 7:24-27 that a house built upon His teachings will stand:

> "Therefore whoever hears these sayings of Mine, and does them, I will liken him to a wise man who built his house on the rock: and the rain descended, the floods came, and the winds blew and beat on that house; and it did not fall, for it was founded on the rock. But everyone who hears these sayings of Mine, and does not do them, will be like a foolish man who built his house on the sand: and the rain descended, the floods came, and the winds blew and beat on that house; and it fell. And great was its fall."

America was built upon a firm foundation of Judeo-Christian values. "The term 'Judeo-Christian' refers to something that has its source in the common foundations of Judaism and Christianity. The Bible includes the Jewish Scriptures of the Old Testament, so the moral foundations laid down in Judaism are upheld in Christianity."[40]

Because our foundation is a firm one, our nation will stand. However, we have weakened our foundation by ungodly laws we have enacted as a nation. To take us back to a healthy foundation, we must repent and repeal. Repent of making these laws in the first place and repeal them for the future of our

---
[40] "What is the Judeo-Christian ethic?," Got Questions.org, Accessed February 4, 2021, www.gotquestions.org/Judeo-Christian-ethic.html.

great nation. It is like the rebuilding of the walls of Jerusalem we read about in the book of Nehemiah. Israel had sinned against God, and they had been taken captive to Babylon. Jerusalem was invaded and parts of it destroyed by King Nebuchadnezzar. Nehemiah appealed to King Artexerxes to return to Jerusalem and rebuild the walls that were destroyed. He was granted favor by the king and was able to travel to Jerusalem to do so. The walls of America have been breached and, in some ways, destroyed because of our sin.

First, let us look at some of the principles upon which this nation was founded. The first document would be the Mayflower Compact, which was written and signed on the *Mayflower* on November 21, 1620. It was the foundational document for the United States of America. Most of the men who braved the rough waters of the Atlantic to make the crossing to the New World would sign this document before they even landed at Plymouth, Massachusetts. It was written with the intention of forming a government, and those who signed it pledged to abide by the laws and regulations that would be established by the new government led by John Carver, who was chosen as the first governor of the new colony.

It was written based upon the Puritan Church Covenant and altered to be used in a civil capacity. In part, the document reads as:

> *Having undertaken, for the Glory of God, and advancements of the Christian faith, and honor of our King and Country, a voyage to plant the first colony in the Northern parts of Virginia; do by these presents, solemnly and mutually, in the presence of God, and one of another, <u>covenant</u> and combine ourselves together into a civil body politic; for our better ordering, and preservation, and furtherance of the ends aforesaid; and by virtue hereof to enact, <u>constitute</u>, and frame, such just and equal laws, ordinances, acts, constitutions, offices, from time to time, as shall be thought most meet and convenient for the general good of the colony; unto which we promise all due submission and obedience.*[41]

---

41 Encyclopedia Brittanica, s.v. "Mayflower Compact," Accessed December 20, 2020, https://www.britannica.com/topic/Mayflower-Compact.

Clearly, as they stated, those who left everything and risked their lives to found a new nation intended that nation to be for the glory of God and to the advancement of the Christian faith. Having laid that out in their original compact, they intended for this new land to do things according to the Word of God, not according to man's dictates. Because they were fleeing from religious persecution in England, they wanted the original intent for the new territory to have religious freedom. They refused to compromise their beliefs. How far we as a nation have fallen from those beliefs—the ones for which they risked their lives.

As a Quaker, William Penn, one of our founding fathers, believed in religious liberty. Penn wanted the new territory he was given to be a refuge for Quakers and others who were experiencing religious persecution. Penn later drew up a Frame of Government for the new colony and insisted on absolute freedom of worship. Two of his famous quotes are, "Men must be governed by God or they will be ruled by tyrants." And "If thou wouldst rule well, thou must rule for God, and to do that, thou must be ruled by him. Those who will not be governed by God will be ruled by tyrants."[42] Clearly, as one of the founding fathers of America, Penn made it clear that God was to be central in the governing of America.

If you graduated from high school in the United States of America, you know these words written within the Declaration of Independence: "We hold these truths to be self-evident, that all men are created equal, that they are endowed by their Creator with certain unalienable Rights, that among these are Life, Liberty, and the pursuit of Happiness."[43] Clearly our founding fathers wanted God and His laws to be an active and vital part of America's government.

In his book *The Way Back*, Dutch Sheets says:

---

42 "William Penn Quotes," AZ Quotes, Accessed December 20, 2020, https://www.az-quotes.com/author/11496-William_Penn.
43 Ibid, 3.

> Knowing the United States of America was God's idea, the framers of our constitution were determined to establish it under His authority and according to His principles. Consider the revealing words of George Washington and John Quincy Adams. "Of all the dispositions and habits which lead to political prosperity, religion and morality are indispensable supports. It is impossible to rightly govern the world without God and the Bible." (George Washington)

> "The highest glory of the American Revolution was this: it connected in one indissoluble bond the principles of civil government with the principles of Christianity." (John Quincy Adams) America was founded in partnership with, and under, God.[44]

The inscription on the Liberty Bell is from the Bible (King James Version):

> "Proclaim Liberty Throughout All the Land Unto All the Inhabitants thereof." This verse refers to the "Jubilee",[sic] or the instructions to the Israelites to return property and free slaves every 50 years. Speaker of the Pennsylvania Assembly Isaac Norris chose this inscription for the State House bell in 1751, possibly to commemorate the 50th anniversary of William Penn's 1701 Charter of Privileges which granted religious liberties and political self-government to the people of Pennsylvania.[45]

The Liberty Bell was housed in the statehouse of Pennsylvania and was used to call the lawmakers to their meetings.

One hundred six of our first 108 colleges have a Christian background. Here is a quote from Harvard's "Rules and Precepts," adopted in 1646:

> Everyone shall consider the main end of his life and studies to know God in Jesus Christ which is eternal life. Seeing the Lord giveth wisdom, everyone shall seriously by prayer in secret seek

---

44 Dutch Sheets, *The Way Back* (2017), 10.
45 "The Liberty Bell," National Park Service.org, Accessed December 20, 2020, www.nps.gov/inde/learn/historyculture/stories-libertybell.htm.

wisdom of him. Everyone should also exercise himself in reading the scriptures twice a day that they be ready to give an account of their proficiency therein, both in theoretical observations of languages and logic, and in practical and spiritual truths.[46]

These examples are just some of the foundational principles that America was built upon. Principles founded upon the Rock, Jesus Christ, so we, as a nation, can stand the floods and winds of life that beat upon us.

However, we have allowed our foundations to be weakened by ungodly laws. One of which is taking prayer out of the schools. When I was in elementary school, we had an older lady who traveled around to the schools in the district with her flannel board, teaching Bible stories and ending in prayer. No one at that time questioned this taking place in the schools. It was not until 1962 that the U.S. Supreme Court declared school-sponsored prayers unconstitutional in the landmark case of *Engel v. Vitale*.[47]

It seems that after prayer was taken out of the schools, terror was allowed into them. It is a biblical principle that when one spirit is removed, another will take its place. "Then he goes and takes with him seven other spirits more wicked than himself, and they enter and dwell there; and the last *state* of that man is worse than the first" (Matt. 12:45). In our case, we allowed the godly spirit of prayer to be removed, and ungodly spirits of terror and death took the place of prayer in our schools. I tried to come up with an accurate number of people killed or wounded in school-related shootings since 1962, but the list was so extensive, I gave up trying to get an accurate count. I was appalled at how many there were, ones of which I had never even heard.

One school shooting will be forever etched in my mind. I was returning from Brazil after being on a mission trip when the news came across in the airport at JFK about the Sandy Hook Elementary School shooting. We had spent

---

46 "How Christians Started the Ivy League," The Forerunner.com, April 6, 2008, www.forerunner.com/forerunner/X0101_Christians_Started_I.html.
47 Charles C. Haynes, "50 Years Later, How School-Prayer Ruling Changed America," July 29, 2012, https://www.freedomforuminstitute.org/2012/07/29/.

more than two days with five flights back-to-back, missing one that backed us up to miss others. We spent one night in a hotel in Brazil, waiting on a newly booked flight from the first one we missed. We also spent one night on the floor at JFK waiting on another substitute flight from a missed one. I say this in defense of how tired we were. My friend and I were also sick. It had been a two-week mission, with little sleep and constantly being on the go. When the news came on, it barely registered what had happened at Sandy Hook. I asked my friend what was going on when I returned from a restroom break and got in on the tail end of the report. Her answer was, "Just another school shooting." That sounds callous under the circumstances, but because they were so frequent in America and because of the state we were in physically, that was the answer at the time. It was not until the next day when I was home and had a good night's sleep that the gravity of what had happened began to register with me. I was as horrified and heartbroken as every other American was, or should have been, over what happened to those precious children; unfortunately, many more would be killed in later school shootings.

Another ungodly law we enacted in America was *Roe v. Wade*, the famous abortion law. On January 22, 1973, the Supreme Court of the United States of America struck down a Texas law that banned abortions. This opened a floodgate for legal abortions to take place in America. Prior to this, abortion had been mainly illegal in the U.S. This law is totally against what the Word of God tells us. To God, all life is valuable, even a life in the womb. Psalm 127:3-5a says, "Behold, children *are* a heritage from the Lord, The fruit of the womb *is* a reward. Like arrows in the hand of a warrior, So *are* the children of one's youth. Happy *is* the man who has his quiver full of them." It does not say only those children who are planned and convenient. And, of course, we all know the sixth commandment: "You shall not murder" (Exod. 20:13). Taking any life, no matter what stage of development it is in, is murder.

The Bible also tells us, "'A man shall leave his father and mother and be joined to his wife, and the two shall become one flesh'" (Matt. 19:5). It also states in Genesis 1:27, "So God created man in His *own* image; in the image of God He created him; male and female He created them." He made them to be joined together to procreate to populate the earth. Two men having sex or two women having sex cannot produce a biological child. God says in 1 Corinthians 6:9-10, "Or do you not know that the unrighteous will not inherit the kingdom of God? Do not be deceived; neither fornicators, nor idolaters, nor adulterers, nor effeminate, nor homosexuals, nor thieves, nor *the* covetous, nor drunkards, nor revilers, nor swindlers will inherit the kingdom of God." God loves all the above people in the categories listed. However, He hates their sin and says they will not inherit the Kingdom of God. God always intended for marriage to be between a man and a woman, never between two men or two women. What did our United States Supreme Court do with this sacred union?

> Writing for the majority, Justice Anthony Kennedy asserted that the right to marry is a fundamental right "inherent in the liberty of the person" and is therefore protected by the due process clause, which prohibits the states from depriving any person of "life, liberty, or property without due process of law." By virtue of the close connection between liberty and equality, the marriage right is also guaranteed by the equal protection clause, which forbids the states from "deny[ing] to any person . . . the equal protection of the laws." Kennedy then argued at length that "the reasons marriage is fundamental, including its connection with individual liberty, apply with equal force to same-sex couples. Such considerations, he concluded, compel the court to hold that "same-sex couples may exercise the fundamental right to marry."[48]

By giving the right to same-sex marriage, America again violated God's moral laws written in His Word. These are only a few examples of America

---

48 *Encyclopedia Britannica*, s.v. "Obergefell v. Hodges," Accessed January 2, 2021, https://www.britannica.com/event/Obergefell-v-Hodges.

turning away from Him and what His Word says. This is not just this writer's opinion; this is what the Word of God says.

America has strayed far from God's original intent for her. The church is guilty of allowing these things to happen. They happened on our watch. Dutch Sheets writes:

> Frenchman Alex de Tocqueville came to America in 1831 to study our nation. Sadly, we have experienced his warning: "I sought for the key to the greatness and genius of America in her harbors; in her fertile fields and boundless forest; in her rich mines and vast world commerce; in her public school system and institutions of learning. I sought for it in her Democratic Congress and in her matchless Constitution. Not until I went into the churches of America and heard her pulpits aflame with righteousness did I understand the secret of her genius and power. America is great because America is good, and if America ever ceases to be good, America will cease to be great."[49]

We are on the brink of ceasing to be great because we are no longer good in so many vital ways.

It is time for us to turn back to Him and to His original intent for this nation, a nation known as a Christian nation, and to rebuild the spiritual walls of America by repealing the laws that put us in the place we are in today, with breaches that have allowed the enemy access to our great county. He has accessed it both spiritually and in reality. In turning back to God, He will again bless us as a nation, but it is up to us to shore up our breached walls with repentance and repealing these ungodly laws.

I close this book with the words from 2 Corinthians 11:3-4 in the Passion Translation (PTP):

> But now I'm afraid that just as Eve was deceived by the serpent's clever lies, your thoughts may be corrupted and you may lose your single-hearted devotion and pure love for Christ. For you seem

---

49 Sheets, 12.

to gladly tolerate anyone who comes to you preaching a pseudo-Jesus, not the Jesus we have preached. You have accepted a spirit and gospel that is false, rather than the Spirit and gospel you once embraced. How tolerant you have become of these imposters!

Let us not be deceived away from the original intent of our Creator, as individuals, as the *ecclesia* (Church), or as a nation.

EPILOGUE

While on the surface all seemed lost after the Fall of mankind, it truly was not because God made a way back to Himself and to paradise through His Son Jesus Christ. Jesus told one of the men hanging next to Him on his own cross that later that day he would be with Jesus in Paradise. "And he was saying, 'Jesus, remember me when You come in Your kingdom!' And He said to him, 'Truly I say to you, today you shall be with Me in Paradise'" (Luke 23:43). One of the terms for paradise in the original Greek means "a garden."[50]

We see this same term again in Revelation 2:7: "He who has an ear, let him hear what the Spirit says to the churches. To him who overcomes, I will grant to eat of the tree of life which is in the Paradise of God.'" Some of Jesus' last recorded words were of having a garden relationship with mankind again. Don't you know He was so looking forward to spending that kind of time and fellowship with the man sharing the same pain and suffering He was going through on the cross? They both could focus on that and not on their suffering, and maybe it lessened their suffering some.

Jesus actually says in Hebrews 12:2, "Fixing our eyes on Jesus, the author and perfecter of faith, who for the joy set before Him endured the cross, despising the shame, and has sat down at the right hand of the throne of God." Is it possible that "the joy set before Him was knowing He would once again be in paradise with His children, enjoying unhindered fellowship with them again? And the shame that entered into the world through Adam and

---

50 *Blue Letter Bible*, s.v. "paradeisos," www.blueletterbible.org/lang/Lexicon/Lexicon.cfm?strongs=G3857&t=KJV (accessed January 1, 2020).

Eve would be the thing that would now be forever banished from the Garden. Shame would never again exist where God dwells with those who know Him as Savior and Lord.

The Godhead so loved Their relationship with Adam and Eve in the Garden that Their desire was not only to forgive our sin and take our infirmities to the cross but also to make a way to restore us to a garden-like, intimate relationship with Them again. We have come full circle back to the place where it all began for mankind—the garden. That place of unimaginable beauty but also the place before sin entered the world and marred the relationship with our Maker. A place where, if we have received Jesus as our Savior, we can once again have unhindered, naked fellowship with Him and not be ashamed. Won't that be glorious!

If you don't know Jesus as your Lord and Savior pray this prayer sincerely from your heart. You must mean it; it cannot be said as if it were an insurance policy.

> *Jesus, I recognize I am a sinner in need of a Savior. I understand that You are the only One Who can save me from my sins and make a way back to the Father because of the blood You shed in going to the cross. I ask You to forgive me of all my sins, and I ask You to come and live within me as my Lord and Savior from this day forward.*

Now seek out an evangelical church to join and learn to grow into the man or woman God called you to be. Please contact me at ldent3@juno.com and let me know of the decision that you made.

May all who have read this book be blessed by the Lord!—Leah

BIBLIOGRAPHY

Andrew, Brother John Sherrill, and Elizabeth Sherrill. *God's Smuggler*. Grand Rapids: Chosen Books, 2001.

Barker, Kenneth, General Ed. "Genesis Introduction." In *Zondervan NASB Study Bible*. Grand Rapids: Zondervan Publishing House, 1999).

Bing.com, s.v., "intent," accessed July 1, 2019, www.bing.com/search?q=intent+meaning&form.

Bing.com, s.v., "original," accessed July 1, 2019, www.bing.com/search?q=original+meaning&form.

Bing.com, s.v., "succour," accessed October 1, 2019, www.bing.com/search?q=succour+definition&form.

Blue Letter Bible, s.v. "arrabōn," accessed August 1, 2019, www.blueletterbible.org/lang/Lexicon/Lexicon.cfm?strongs=G728&t=KJV.

Blue Letter Bible, s.v. "bara'," accessed December 3, 2019, www.blueletterbible.org/lang/Lexicon/Lexicon.cfm?strongs=H1254&t=KJV.

Blue Letter Bible, s.v. "doxa," accessed October 1, 2019, www.blueletterbible.org/lang/Lexicon/Lexicon.cfm?strongs=G1391&t=KJV.

Blue Letter Bible, s.v. "ezer," accessed October 1, 2019, www.blueletterbible.org/lang/Lexicon/Lexicon.cfm?strongs=H5828&t=KJV.

Blue Letter Bible, s.v., "garash," accessed August 1, 2019, www.blueletterbible.org/lang/Lexicon/Lexicon.cfm?strongs=H1644&t=KJV.

Blue Letter Bible, s.v. "itstsabown," accessed August 1, 2019, www.blueletterbible.org/lang/Lexicon/Lexicon.cfm?strongs=H6093&t=KJV.

Blue Letter Bible, s.v. "kaleō," accessed September 1, 2019, www.blueletterbible.org/lang/Lexicon/Lexicon.cfm?strongs=G2564&t=KJV.

Blue Letter Bible, s.v. "ma'kob," accessed August 1, 2019, www.blueletterbible.org/lang/Lexicon/Lexicon.cfm?strongs=H4341&t=KJV.

Blue Letter Bible, s.v. "memshalah," accessed December 1, 2019, www.blueletterbible.org/lang/Lexicon/Lexicon.cfm?strongs=H4475&t=NASB.

Blue Letter Bible, s.v., "nephesh," accessed August 1, 2019, www.blueletterbible.org/lang/Lexicon/Lexicon.cfm?strongs=H5315&t=KJV.

Blue Letter Bible, s.v. "něshamah," accessed August 1, 2019, www.blueletterbible.org/lang/Lexicon/Lexicon.cfm?strongs=H5397&t=KJV.

Blue Letter Bible, s.v. "paradeisos," accessed January 1, 2020, www.blueletterbible.org/lang/Lexicon/Lexicon.cfm?strongs=G3857&t=KJV.

Blue Letter Bible, s.v. "psyche," accessed August 1, 2019, www.blueletterbible.org/lang/Lexicon/Lexicon.cfm?strongs=G5590&t=KJV.

Blue Letter Bible, s.v., "re'shiyth," accessed July 1, 2019, www.blueletterbible.org/lang/Lexicon/Lexicon.cfm?strongs=H7225&t=KJV.

Blue Letter Bible, s.v. "yada," accessed August 1, 2019, www.blueletterbible.org/lang/Lexicon/Lexicon.cfm?strongs=H3045&t=KJV.

Cahn, Jonathan. The Book of Mysteries. Lake Mary: Frontline, 2016.

CBN News. "Teen Transgender: 'I Feel As Though I Have Ruined My Life.'" Intercessors for America. Accessed December 1, 2019. https://www.ifapray.org/blog/teen-transgender-i-feel-as-though-i-have-ruined-my-life/.

Culbertson, Patricia, Editor. Smith Wigglesworth Devotional. New Kensington: Whitaker House, 1999.

Foster, John. "Church History: Constantine, an Emperor Who Defied God." Church of God. Accessed August 1, 2019. https://lifehopeandtruth.com/change/the-church/church-history-constantine.

Encyclopedia Brittanica, s.v. "Mayflower Compact." Accessed December 20, 2020. https://www.britannica.com/topic/Mayflower-Compact.

Encyclopedia Britannica, s.v. "Obergefell v. Hodges." Accessed January 2, 2021. https://www.britannica.com/event/Obergefell-v-Hodges.

Free Dictionary, The, s.v. "plomb." Accessed July 1, 2019. www.thefreedictionary.com/plomb.

Hayford, Jack W., Editor. "Kingdom Dynamics: Before the Fall." In *Spirit-Filled Life Bible: NKJV*. Nashville: Thomas Nelson, 1991.

Hayford, Jack W., Editor. *Word Wealth-Jh.1:5*, s.v. "comprehend." In *Spirit-Filled Life Bible NKJV*. Nashville: Thomas Nelson, 1991.

Hayford, s.v. "heychal."

Hayford, s.v. "marturion."

Hayford, s.v. "scotia."

Haynes, Charles C. "50 Years Later, How School-Prayer Ruling Changed America." July 29, 2012. https://www.freedomforuminstitute.org/2012/07/29.

"How Christians Started the Ivy League." The Forerunner.com. April 6, 2008. www.forerunner.com/forerunner/X0101_Christians_Started_I.html.

"Liberty Bell, The." National Park Service.org. Accessed December 20, 2020. www.nps.gov/inde/learn/historyculture/stories-libertybell.htm.

PNW Staff. "Children on The Front Lines: 10 Terrifying Examples of LGBT Indoctrination." Prophecy News Watch. Accessed December 3, 2019. https://www.prophecynewswatch.com/article.cfm?recent_news_id=3622.

Schaeffer, Edith. *Christianity is Jewish.* Wheaton: Tyndale House Publishers, 1975.

Schaser, Nicholas J. "Did Eve Come from Adam's Rib?" Israel Bible Weekly. Accessed September 27, 2019. https://weekly.israelbiblecenter.com/eve-come-adams-rib.

Sheets, Dutch. *The Way Back.* 2017.

Stonestreet, John. "Transgenderism & The Emperor's New Clothes." Prophecy News Watch. Accessed December 3, 2019. https://www.prophecynewswatch.com/article.cfm?recent_news_id=3629.

Strong's Hebrew Lexicon, s.v. "kabed." Accessed October 1, 2019. www.eliyah.com/cgi-bin/strongs.cgi?file=hebrewlexicon&isindex=3513.

"Tract 22B: The Story of Constantine—The Man Who Changed the Christian Church—Supplement to Lesson 22." Champsoftruth.com. Accessed August 1, 2019. http://www.champs-of-truth.com/lessons/tract_22b.htm.

"What is the Judeo-Christian ethic?" Got Questions.org. Accessed February 4, 2021. www.gotquestions.org/Judeo-Christian-ethic.html.

"William Penn Quotes." *AZ Quotes.* Accessed December 20, 2020. https://www.azquotes.com/author/11496-William_Penn.

Zodhiates, Spiros Ed. "Genesis." In *Hebrew-Greek Key Study Bible NASB.* Chattanooga: AMG Publishers, 1990.

DISCOGRAPHY

Jesus Culture, *Live from New York*. Integrity Music. 1-8. 2012, compact disc.

Wilbur, Paul. *The Watchman*. Hosanna! Music. 6. 2005

For more information about
Leah Augustine Dent
and
Gensis of Original Intent
please visit:

www.leahaugustinedent.com

Ambassador International's mission is to magnify the Lord Jesus Christ and promote His Gospel through the written word.

We believe through the publication of Christian literature, Jesus Christ and His Word will be exalted, believers will be strengthened in their walk with Him, and the lost will be directed to Jesus Christ as the only way of salvation.

For more information about
AMBASSADOR INTERNATIONAL
please visit:

www.ambassador-international.com
@AmbassadorIntl
www.facebook.com/AmbassadorIntl

Thank you for reading this book. Please consider leaving us a review on your social media, favorite retailer's website, Goodreads or Bookbub, or our website.

More from Ambassador International

Whether we realize it or not, we all have an internal belief system—a worldview—which directs our thoughts and actions. Our worldview is how we understand the world around us—where we came from, how we should live, and what our purpose is. Examining your personal worldview in light of God's Master Story can strengthen your faith and clarify your purpose in this world.

In *Transformed Thinking*, Tom Wheeler clearly lays out the most fundamental beliefs of Christianity and compares them to other worldviews, providing arguments to support his beliefs. Even though this book is purposed for the classroom setting, it would be a beneficial read for any believer who wants to have a firm foundation on which to share their beliefs with unbelievers.

In this powerful work, Dr. Wiles shares eighteen insights for learning how to pray, handle our anger, love our enemies, overcome worry, have a healthy marriage, and so much more. Included are questions for personal reflection or group discussions. *Don't Just Live ... Really Live* offers a practical approach for discerning how to live out the Bible in today's world.

www.ingramcontent.com/pod-product-compliance
Lightning Source LLC
LaVergne TN
LVHW051501070426
835507LV00022B/2878